Better Communication

And How to Achieve It

Better Communication
And How to Achieve It

Sheila Hoctor
and
Karina Lynn

educate.ie

PUBLISHED BY:

Educate.ie

Walsh Educational Books Ltd

Castleisland, Co. Kerry, Ireland

www.educate.ie

EDITOR:

Eileen O'Carroll

PRODUCTION EDITOR:

Kieran O'Donoghue

DESIGN:

Anú Design, Co. Meath

PRINTED AND BOUND BY:

Walsh Colour Print, Castleisland

ISBN: 978-1-907772-58-0

Acknowledgements

We would both like to thank Myrna Egan, who made many constructive criticisms and suggestions that helped Karina and I present this book in a more relevant way. We would also like to thank Eoghan O'Sullivan for contributing a short story and a critique of nature poetry to this text, and Shane Brophy for contributing his thoughts on the character of local journalism.

I would like to thank Brendan O'Loughlin, CEO Offaly Local Development Company, for seeing the value in creating a book like this and for encouraging me to be innovative in compiling my part of it, and John O'Regan, who put forward the idea of this book to begin with. Thanks too to Monica Larkin, who made an immense contribution to the structure of Units 1 and 3.

I would like to thank Toastmasters for contributing to my own ability to communicate with people. I thank my family for their support and encouragement, my husband Michael, my daughters Pauline and Mairead, my sons John, Michael, Andrew and James. Finally, I would like to thank my mother, Ellen Shortall, for teaching me the value of commitment and courage, attributes that stood me in good stead when making this contribution.

Sheila Hoctor

I would like to thank Kieran Fuller for his time and patience in reading parts of the text and providing valuable suggestions and advice.

I would particularly like to thank John O'Regan for seeing in me the ability to take on this challenge.

Finally, and most of all, I would like to thank my family for their motivation, encouragement and ongoing support, particularly my partner, John Mulvihill, my mother, Lily, and my father, John.

Karina Lynn

CONTENTS

Introduction

Our success in life depends to a large extent on how well we communicate, and how we respond to the messages being communicated to us. We wrote this book to help you to discover your own communication skills and to learn to use them better.

It is important to understand the fundamentals of communication if you are to communicate more effectively. We believe that being aware of how our attitudes influence the way we express ourselves is one of the most important lessons we can learn here. Our thoughts translate into behaviour; this in turn converts into messages, through our words, our tone of voice and our body language. As a result, our attitudes permeate all our communications and affect all our relationships. Realising this is crucially important to understanding how we communicate with others and how we respond to the different communications we receive every day.

In Units 1 and 3, we explore these personal skills of speaking, listening, and presenting ourselves to others, both in personal and professional situations. In Unit 2, we focus on written communication. Here you will learn how to communicate through personal letters, business letters, reports and professional documents. There is also an extensive examination of research methods and survey design. We dedicate a chapter to the report and how it should be constructed, using practical examples. We felt that this was particularly worthwhile as the report is worth one-quarter of the marks for the FETAC Communications Level 5 module.

The last unit of the book deals with information technology, and we can hardly overstate its importance. The internet, the mobile phone, smart phone, personal digital assistant and the computer are rapidly changing the way the world communicates. We look at how information technology impacts on our personal and working lives, and devote one full section to the role of social networking websites. We also look at the legislation which covers this area.

The content of this course handbook we believe meets the criteria set out for the FETAC Communications Level 5 module. More than that, communications is a core module in many areas, and we are confident that the knowledge gained here will help you in many other modules, as well as in many life situations.

We hope you enjoy this book, and that you will participate in the exercises so that you will learn from it in a concrete way. Remember, better communication skills can only be achieved by practising them.

Learning happens best when you test yourself, and dare to overcome the challenges life puts before you. We're sure you can meet the challenge of communicating well with the world around you. For our own part, we hope this book will help you on your way.

MAIN LEARNING OUTCOMES

Learners will be able to:

- understand key terms used in communications theory
- recognise the kinds of listening required in different contexts
- demonstrate a range of listening behaviours appropriate to the context
- practise communication techniques relevant to different situations in work and leisure
- participate effectively in group discussion and negotiated decision making
- co-operate and contribute effectively in formal meetings
- prepare and deliver an oral presentation and answer questions on it.

Unit 1

Listening and Speaking

SECTION 1
Communications Theory

Learning Outcomes

Learners will:
- understand the role of sender and receiver in the communication process
- understand the key terms that add value or take from the communication of the message
- understand the relationship between attitude and communication.

Introduction

Communication is an ongoing process. It is the medium used by humans to interact with each other. All forms of communication require a sender, a message and a receiver. 'Communication is a process that involves the exchange of information, thoughts, ideas and emotions. It is a process that involves a sender who encodes and sends the message, which is then carried via the communication channel to the receiver where the receiver decodes the message, processes the information and sends an appropriate reply via the same communication channel' (Manohar, 2009). The theory of communication is important as it gives us a greater understanding of the process involved in every communication

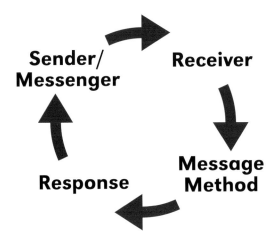

transaction. It explains how the style and attitude of the sender and the receiver can have a positive or negative impact on how a message is communicated.

We are transmitters and receivers of messages, and we often transmit and receive simultaneously. We are constantly transmitting messages in a variety of different ways and with different intensities and intentions. Our communication process involves listening, thinking and speaking and through these processes we continually receive and deliver millions of messages.

Attitudes and behaviour

Understanding attitudes reveals the powerful influence of body language, tone of voice and words in the communication process. All of our behaviours are, in effect, intended or unintended messages.

Let us examine our attitudes, because our behaviours are born from them. As all of our behaviours are messages, too, by examining our behaviours we will be able to identify why we act in a certain way and communicate in an assertive, aggressive or passive manner.

Communication between two or more people involves transactions. One person sends a 'stimulus' (for example a statement or a question) and a response follows. The two taken together constitute a transaction.

Think of all the transactions you engage in each day: conversations, enquiries, complaints, compliments, giving feedback. Sometimes the transaction is one-to-one and sometimes it occurs in a group situation, such as a formal or an informal meeting.

Parent Ego State	Controlling parent	Nurturing parent	**Whole Personality**
Adult Ego State	Adult		
Child Ego State	Natural child	Adapted child	Rebellious child	

Eric Berne developed Transactional Analysis (TA) in the 1950s. He studied how people responded to different stimuli in interpersonal communication. According to Berne, everyone's personality can be analysed in terms of three sub-personalities, which he called ego states: parent, adult and child.

The parent ego state is often sub-divided into nurturing parent and controlling parent. The child ego state is often sub-divided into rebellious, adapted and natural child.

Sometimes a 'stimulus' provokes a response that was not intended by the sender of the message. As a result the mood of the person changes to reflect their ego state. The facial expression and body language demonstrates that the receiver of the message has reacted in a way that has caused upset, insult or pain of some kind.

The sender of the message may be unaware of the effect of the 'stimulus' and may be confused about the reason for the mood swing. But body language reveals that the 'stimulus' has triggered a reaction in the listener that was not intended.

Sometimes the 'stimulus' is fuelled by implication, not words, and the sender can imply a message through their body language. The listener picks up the clues through the sender's body language and reacts to the visible message. This fuels different emotions in the listener.

Depending on our attitude at any time, we slip in and out of different ego states.

The controlling parent ego state may well use words that show their authority: 'I don't/can't/must,' 'That's not good enough,' etc.

When a controlling parent uses words like 'You must,' they can provoke a fireworks response in someone who is in the rebellious child ego state. This crossed transaction can be compounded by the gestures used by the sender in the controlling parent ego state (for example, finger wagging, frowning) and as a result a reaction is triggered in the person who is in the rebellious child ego state. This may manifest itself in sulking, slamming doors and other behaviour that is not appropriate in adult life.

The very same words coming from a controlling parent ego state will provoke a different reaction if the receiver is in the adapted child ego state. This person may want the approval of the controlling parent and be willing to take orders that are inappropriate in the situation.

The nurturing parent ego state may send complimentary messages, as they want to encourage the recipient. They might use language that is encouraging, such as 'Well done,' 'I'm so proud of you,' etc. The body language used is most likely a smile, clapping the person on the back, or maybe clapping their hands or shaking the other person's hand while congratulating them.

The person in the rebellious child ego state may see this as too much fuss and may react in a flippant way – 'So what?' – or may not respond at all to the compliments being sent.

The person in the adapted child ego state may accept the compliments – even if they may be cringing with embarrassment. The trouble with the nurturing parent ego state is that the messages can be over the top and as a result the adapted child can be smothered in the transaction. The best outcome is to modify behaviour to that which is more appropriate.

In the adult ego state we send a stimulus using objectivity and rational thinking, without bias or prejudice. The recipient in the adult ego state can respond in the appropriate way, as the ego states match and the message intended will be the message received. This transaction is unlikely to be loaded with inappropriate gestures, as the person is sending the stimulus based on object-ivity, and the person responding is taking the message sent and evaluating it, seeking out the facts and responding in an appropriate manner.

The ego state of the receiver can have a profound outcome on the communi-cation transaction.

EXAMPLES

Here is an example of a simple question interpreted in a number of different ways, depending on the ego state of the recipient.

Adult to adult: 'Could we meet tomorrow at 2.30 p.m. to prepare an agenda for our residents' meeting?'
Adult to adult: 'That time is fine with me,' *or* 'That time doesn't suit me; how about 3.30 p.m. instead?'
This example provides a simple answer to a simple question; it is straightforward and uncomplicated. This is the kind of behaviour we expect in an adult environment.

However, the response depends on the ego state of the person receiving the message. As a result, messages that should be straightforward can become unintentionally complicated and can cause conflict and difficulties in an organisation or business.

Adult to adult: 'Could we meet tomorrow at 2.30 p.m. to prepare an agenda for our residents' meeting?'
Adapted child to controlling parent: 'You expect me to be available at a moment's notice!'
In this example, the same stimulus is provided but because it is perceived and interpreted through a different ego state, the response is entirely different.

Adult to adult: 'Could we meet tomorrow at 2.30 p.m. to prepare an agenda for our residents' meeting?'

Natural child to controlling parent: 'You must be joking, I have better things to be doing.'

Again, this example provides the same stimulus but because it is interpreted through a different ego state, it results in a different reaction.

Adult to adult: 'Could we meet tomorrow at 2.30 p.m. to prepare an agenda for our residents' meeting?'

Rebellious child: 'Oh, how boring; let's go out for a few drinks.'

Again, a different response to the same stimulus.

Exercise

Which ego state is likely to have the most productive outcome?

Consider the dialogue about the residents' meeting above, and act out body language that is appropriate to each exchange.

Basic Attitudes

We can use the TA model to help us understand the relationship between attitude and behaviour. The terms used are: I = 'I', U = 'You'; they can be positive (+) or negative (−).

How we send and receive messages depends on our attitudes. With the right attitude we build both professional and personal relationships. We resolve conflict situations in a fair and impartial way. We solve problems by seeking the input of others and then making an informed decision. We build effective teams in which respect for the individual member is important, as well as achieving the best possible result.

I+ U+ (assertive)

I'm OK and you're OK, therefore I value me and I value you. As a result, when I+ sends a message, I+ sends it in a clear and concise way. When a U+ person receives a message, U+ listens carefully to the sender and if necessary clarifies with the sender that the message that he/she sent was the message that was received. Therefore, both needs are met.

I– U+ (passive)

I believe I'm not OK and you're OK. Therefore, in this situation, the I– person will not be confident enough to send clear, unambiguous messages and the receiver will most likely need to question the I– person in order to understand what the message means. Therefore it is more difficult to interpret the message and oftentimes the real message can get lost in the sending. It is more difficult for the U+ person in this case to be sure that the message sent was the message received.

I+ U– (aggressive)

The I+ person feels that they are OK but the U– person is not OK. The I+ person sees himself as better than the U– person and as a result may talk down to the U– person. The I+ person may speak in an angry tone of voice and make the U– person feel inferior. As a result, a clear message is unlikely to be received by the U– person because it is loaded with anger.

I– U– (avoiding)

The I– person feels that they are not OK and that the U– person is not OK either. As a result, they might never try to communicate clearly as they feel it is too much bother and generally the I– person's message tends to be complaining.

Exercises

1. Describe how different attitudes might affect the sender.

2. Describe how different attitudes might affect the receiver.

3. Pick out statements from the following list and relate them to the different attitudes just discussed.

   (a) Puts others down.

   (b) Makes statements that are brief, clear and to the point.

   (c) Must be a winner at another's expense.

   (d) Eager to please others all the time.

   (e) Makes good use of 'I' statements.

   (f) Unwilling and unable to say no.

(g) 'I'll get nowhere with that.'

(h) 'I think,' 'I believe,' 'I hope,' etc.

(i) Always apologising for their actions.

(j) Gets annoyed and loses their temper.

(k) Thinks others must be right and they must be wrong.

(l) Distinguishes between fact and opinion.

(m) Hides own feelings.

(n) 'My opinion is ...'

(o) Thinks it's not worth the bother.

(p) Makes long rambling statements justifying themselves.

(q) 'It's a waste of time.'

(r) States their opinions as facts: 'That's rubbish,' 'That idea will never work.'

(s) Uses phrases that make it easy for others to ignore their views: 'It's not important, but ...,' 'I only meant ...'

(t) Avoids 'should,' 'must,' 'ought.'

(u) Uses threats: 'You'd better get on with it,' 'I wouldn't do that if I were you.'

Passive	Aggressive	Assertive	Avoiding
I– U+	I+ U–	I+ U+	I– U–

Personality

Aggressive Person	Passive Person	Assertive Person	Avoiding Person
↓	↓	↓	↓
Own worst enemy; others avoid working with this type of person. They sometimes cause uproar in an organisation as they tend to put the blame on others.	Could be a doormat for others because of inability to stand up for self. You don't know how their thinking works. They avoid issues, are unlikely to take initiative and are constantly looking for approval.	You know exactly where you stand with this type of person. They are as honest as the day is long. They are often described as people that shine in their personal and professional life.	Lacks motivation and will always make excuses not to participate in activities. They merely exist. A typical statement from this type of person might be, 'It's an awful old world we are living in.'
↓	↓	↓	↓
Manipulative	Submissive	Takes Ownership	Too Much Bother
↓	↓	↓	↓
Relationships are turbulent and sometimes disrespectful. They tend to blame others.	Relationships are built on fear and undervaluing their contribution.	Relationships are built on trust and respect. They value the opinions of others.	Relationships are withdrawn. They are often suspicious of others.

Which weather reflects how you communicate your message?

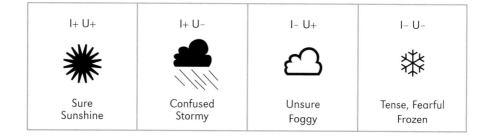

I+ U+	I+ U−	I− U+	I− U−
Sure Sunshine	Confused Stormy	Unsure Foggy	Tense, Fearful Frozen

Do you need to change your attitude?

How do you come across to other people?

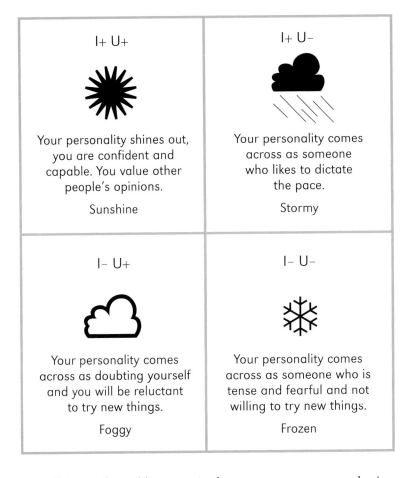

I+ U+	I+ U−
Your personality shines out, you are confident and capable. You value other people's opinions. Sunshine	Your personality comes across as someone who likes to dictate the pace. Stormy
I− U+	I− U−
Your personality comes across as doubting yourself and you will be reluctant to try new things. Foggy	Your personality comes across as someone who is tense and fearful and not willing to try new things. Frozen

Our personalities are formed by our attitudes, our ego states, our enthusiasm, our energy, our interest, our values and the way we communicate our feelings and interact with the people around us. Our personalities are also influenced by our childhood experiences, the way we explore the world around us and the way we react to the circumstances we find ourselves in. Some people are risk takers and some people are risk averse. Some people are leaders and some are followers. The level of confidence we develop as human beings often depends on whether we are prepared to move out of our comfort zones and dare to risk becoming all that we are capable of being.

I+ U+	I+ U−
'What you see is what you get'	'On your high horse'
I− U+	I− U−
'In disguise'	'The weight of the world'

Tone of voice

What clues to our state of mind do we provide in our tone of voice?

- We provide clues about our sincerity, our conviction, our enthusiasm and our passion for a particular situation, subject or event.
- We can equally show indifference, hostility and harshness.
- We can show how excited we are about an event.
- We can be abrupt and impatient in tone when we are in a belittling mood or if someone is getting on our nerves.

- We can be monotonous and lifeless when we are totally uninterested in a subject or event.
- We have clarity in our tone of voice when we are open and clear in the way we express our opinions.
- We can show respect for our fellow human beings by the tone of voice we use, whether it is helpful, encouraging, friendly, empathetic or professional.

The words we use are one thing, but we can communicate a very different meaning through our tone. Not surprisingly, the reaction we get can be different depending on the intention of the speaker and the clues that the listener picks up from the speaker's tone.

Our manner and tone of voice can have an important role in the outcome of most communication situations.

Exercise

1. Think about how someone will express their opinion depending on whether they:
   - behave in a superior way (I+ U–)
   - behave in an inferior way (I– U+)
   - treat other people as equals (I+ U+)
   - appear to be indifferent (I– U–)

   How will their tone of voice be different?

2. Using the appropriate tone of voice and body language, create and act out a script using the kind of words that are appropriate to each attitude.

   What did you learn from this exercise?

   How does the receiver of the message react to the different behaviours?

   Is it different depending on where they are in the quadrant themselves?

3. What kind of body language, tone of voice and words would you expect from each of the following?

	I+ U+	I– U+	I+ U–	I– U–
Body Language				
Tone of Voice				
Words				

Summary

'Sow an act. You reap a habit.
Sow a habit. You reap a character.
Sow a character. You reap a destiny.'
(George Boardman the Younger)

Looking at this quotation and applying it to the communication process, we can see that we influence others, for better or worse, depending on the type of behaviour we engage in. The messages we send to others, the tone of voice we use and the body language we demonstrate determines the quality of the relationships we build with others.

The concept of ego states may suggest a possible explanation as to why so many communication transactions go askew and that the ego states of both sender and receiver have a direct bearing on the outcome. Managers in all walks of life say they require people with the right attitude. They are aware that they will be able to express their opinions and solve problems in the adult ego state and the person receiving the message will be capable of objectivity and will draw on logic and not emotion in formulating their response. This will make for a more productive and pleasant atmosphere, whether it is a work environment, a meeting environment or a team sport environment.

As we have seen, however, that ideal is rarely achieved in reality.

Sensory variation

Channels of communication

Channels of communication comprise all our senses and we can make our communication process more meaningful and more valuable if we reach people through their preferred channel. These channels are:

- visual (images)
- auditory (words and sounds)
- kinaesthetic (feelings and sensations)
- olfactory (smells)
- gustatory (tastes).

Identifying another person's preferred sensory channel gives us the opportunity to speak in their language and build a rapport with them.

EXAMPLE

The restaurant

Lots of restaurant owners try to incorporate many channels of communication into their businesses. The aim is to give a 'total experience' to their customers. This helps customers to indulge their senses, absorb the ambience and savour the experience.

In the restaurant experience we are first aware of the surroundings. We often hear people say that the surroundings were idyllic. The presentation of the staff and the presentation of the food must be in keeping with our first impressions. Background music can add value, as can the way the staff meet and greet us and how they speak with us throughout the experience. Feelings can be communicated through a number of different channels: people, surroundings, sound, music and colour.

The experience can also be made more memorable by, for example, the hot and cold sensations presented through a combination of different food. The aroma of the food can intensify our hunger and can add to the experience. A subtle presentation of flowers such as lilies or roses can add value through their scent and visual impact. The different tastes of the food will provide the ultimate dining experience. If all these senses can be indulged the customer will regard the restaurant highly and will most likely come back and recommend it to friends. As a result, an excellent rapport will be built with customers.

We filter information through a number of channels. We all have our preferred channels and that is why, when we use a variety of different channels, we allow more people to filter the message in the most appropriate way for them. We can engage their interest and establish a rapport with them by tuning into their preferred channel.

Describing multiple sensory input, neurologist Lawrence Katz comments: 'Anything that uses all your senses to do something forms associations that makes the brain more fit and agile.'

Exercise

How can you add value to your message by using more channels of communication?

Summary

The quality of our relationships is determined by the quality of our communication skills. The following skills and attributes are essential to good interpersonal relationships:

- positive attitude
- assertive behaviour
- pro-active listening
- effective questions
- appropriate body language
- empathy
- appropriate tone of voice
- encoding the message
- thinking about the appropriate response by decoding the message
- using words in a clear and concise way to give and receive information.

Our attitude permeates all aspects of interpersonal communication. Therefore, it is the foundation stone in building effective personal and professional relation-ships. It is the root cause of our behaviour.

Listening

Learning Outcomes

Learners will:

- recognise listening as a key skill to foster in understanding and obtaining better information
- recognise that with better listening behaviours, better relationships can be built.

'An essential part of true listening is the discipline of setting aside one's own prejudices, frames of reference and desires so as to experience the speaker's world from the inside.'

(M. Scott Peck, *The Road Less Travelled*)

Introduction

Listening is an active skill that requires the listener to listen to what the speaker means, not just to hear what the speaker says. We listen on many different levels and for many different reasons. We listen to understand, to interpret meaning and to receive information. We spend a large part of our waking time listening.

Understanding: being in tune with the speaker, not just listening to the words they are saying, but interpreting their tone of voice and body language. This will help to extract the meaning of the message and its overall context.

Interpreting: being able to decode the information. Interpreting also involves being able to simplify the information – explaining it in a simpler way without changing the meaning – such as when we read and then make sense of, for example, legal contracts.

Receiving information: being able to listen to information, extract the facts and make sure that they are correct, as this is generally not open to interpretation. For example, if you are told by your doctor to take 5 ml of a particular medicine, you need to receive that important information correctly. You can learn a lot by listening in the appropriate way.

Listening well provides a foundation for effective personal and business relationships. The listener needs to commit to the listening process, to take the time to listen to the relevant information, and to respond appropriately to the other person.

The following chart shows the worthwhile conversions that can come about through effective listening.

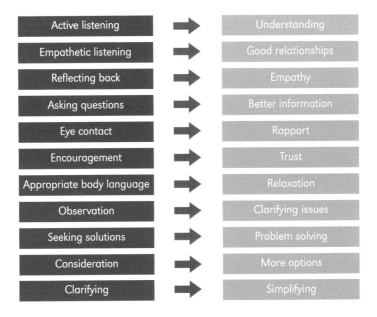

Active listening	Understanding
Empathetic listening	Good relationships
Reflecting back	Empathy
Asking questions	Better information
Eye contact	Rapport
Encouragement	Trust
Appropriate body language	Relaxation
Observation	Clarifying issues
Seeking solutions	Problem solving
Consideration	More options
Clarifying	Simplifying

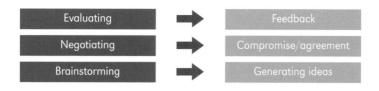

Evaluating	➡	Feedback
Negotiating	➡	Compromise/agreement
Brainstorming	➡	Generating ideas

'On Listening'

When I ask you to listen to me and you start giving me advice, you have not done what I have asked.

When I ask you to listen to me and you begin to tell me why I shouldn't feel that way, you are trampling on my feelings.

When I ask you to listen to me and you feel you have to do something to solve my problem, you have failed me, strange as that may seem.

Listen, all I asked was that you listen, not to talk or do – just to hear me.

Advice is cheap; a few pence will get both. Dear John, or Joan, in the same newspaper. And I do, do for myself, I am not helpless, maybe discouraged and faltering but not helpless.

When you do something for me that I can and need to do for myself, you contribute to my fear and inadequacy. But when you accept as a simple fact that I do feel what I feel, no matter how irrational, then I can quit trying to convince you and get about the business of understanding what's behind this irrational feeling.

And when that's clear, the answers are obvious and I don't need advice.

Irrational feelings make sense when we understand what's behind them, perhaps that's why prayer works sometimes – for some people. Because God *is mute and he doesn't give advice or try to fix things. He listens and lets you work it out for yourself.*

So please listen and just hear me, and if you want to talk, wait a minute for your turn and I'll listen to you.

Anonymous

Exercise

If you were the author of 'On Listening', how would you like the listener to react?

Active listening

Active listening is not just about listening, it is about leaving the speaker in no doubt that they have been heard. As an active listener:

- you are also aware of the intensity with which the words are spoken
- you are aware of body language and tone
- your listening acknowledges the emotions and needs of the other
- you decide what emotion has been sent and put it into words
- you acknowledge any problem and help the speaker to break it down by reflection and asking appropriate questions.

Here are some pointers to finding solutions using the basic skills of active listening (notice the non-verbal communications in the listening process).

- Always remember that if you are fully listening, you are fully concentrating on what the person is saying (eye contact and facial expression).
- You are checking with the person that what you thought you heard is what the speaker meant (testing understanding).
- You are giving the person the opportunity to put it a different way (encouraging).
- You are breaking down the components of the conversation; for example, if the person is saying that they have a problem, you are identifying by questioning the person further (testing understanding).

- Which part is the problem for the person? (encouraging).
- What could they do to bring about a better outcome? (encouraging).
- Ask pertinent questions, such as 'If I understand you right, is this the piece of the problem that is holding you back?' (testing understanding).
- Summarise at different intervals so that the person is in no doubt that you are fully listening and that you have heard the essence of their words (encouraging).
- A good listener helps the person unravel their thinking by breaking down the different elements of the conversation and reflecting back what they heard (reflecting back and understanding).
- Ask the person what they mean if you are not sure: 'You say that you feel people expect too much from you. Can you quantify the impact of that on you?' (testing understanding).
- Ask 'What if …?' to allow the person to explore other options (encouraging).
- Act as the listening mirror (reflecting back).
- Keep the discussion on track (control of own responses).
- Give the speaker your whole self (encouraging).
- Don't assume you know their answer (control of own responses).
- If you are talking you can't be listening (control of own responses).
- Don't interrupt (control of own responses).

When listening skills are examined closely it is very obvious that, apart from hearing the words that are said, very much of the listening process involves body language and tone of voice.

We use listening skills to take instruction, to answer questions, to clarify information. Good listening skills are key to successful relationships, to problem solving, to closing sales, to good customer services, to being successful in job interviews. Often, previously unknown options become available to the person. Two heads are better than one. However, when a good listener is listening with all of the senses, the impact is truly immense.

Exercise

Refer back to Berne's TA model as described in Section 1. Look again at attitudes and their relevance to listening skills and suggest the different approaches listeners might take, depending on their attitude.

Tips for listening effectively

- We need to listen with our mind and our body.
- We need to suspend judgement.
- We need to keep an open mind.
- We need to give the speaker our full attention.
- We need to ask questions.
- We need to want to understand.
- We need to observe what is being said.
- We need to use appropriate body language.
- We need to be sincere and honest.
- We need to give our time.
- We need to let the speaker talk.
- We need to listen to what is not being said.
- We need to close our mouths and avoid interruptions except to give feedback.
- We need to let the speaker know that we are listening and that we want to listen.

We are living in an era when we can get information at the touch of a button. Perhaps that is why we feel we can access all the answers. However, it is more necessary than ever to listen attentively to our fellow human beings as we may well need their wisdom and understanding to solve the problems of today's society. We also have many lonely people who need to connect with other people. When we listen attentively to a person we connect with that person. Real communication is all about connection.

Why is listening so important?

Through listening we acquire new information and new thinking. As a result, we can make informed decisions. We can build on the information that we already have, we can resolve problems, clarify issues and find new and better ways of doing things. As a result, we can be more creative in our thinking and we can design new products and services. We can build better relationships as each person knows that their input is valuable.

'When people talk, listen completely. Most people never listen.'
(Ernest Hemingway)

Exercise

Receiving Information

1. Three people leave the room and the following passage is read to a person who stays behind to listen and repeat the message to one of those who have gone outside. The people outside are invited back one at a time. The first one is told the story, and he/she passes it on to the next in line. They pass it on in turn. The message is:

    Mary comes from a large family. She is the second eldest of nine children, seven girls and two boys. The children are very close in age as there are only thirteen years between the oldest and the youngest. They were born in the following months: one in January, one in March, one in April, two in May, two in June, one in September and one in November.

After doing the exercise, reflect on these issues:

Did the story change much?
Why/why not?
What have we learned about our listening skills?
What have we learned about how we present information?
How can we improve the way we present information?
How can we learn to listen better?
Can losing the message be as much the fault of the presenter as the listener?

This piece is full of facts, which could be a turn-off for some listeners. Using a simpler version, it is much more likely that the information will be heard and understood by the listener.

2. Which of these words would you associate with good listening skills?
    Open, closed, recognition, advocate, annoy, apathy, acknowledge, assume, undermine, prejudices, respect, understanding, contact, judgemental, equals, hear, clash, simple, watching, meaning, trust, attention, alert, content, concentrate, interruption, explain, solve, allow, ask, notice, encourage, pause, validate, clarify, distractions, assimilate, interjection, question, non-threatening, criticising, pretending, evaluating, restate.

3. How can you improve the quality of your speaking so that you are more likely to be listened to?

Listening to chat shows

Have you ever listened to a chat show on radio or television and been enthralled by the interviewee?

He/she has an amazing story to tell. You are really tuned in. The content and delivery really appeal to you. However, you are really disappointed when the interviewer asks questions that have been answered already and now, due to time constraints, you don't get to hear as much as you want on a particular subject or story. Also, an obvious question comes up as a result of something said and the interviewer doesn't pick up on it. Instead they ask a totally unrelated question.

The interviewer interrupts the speaker unnecessarily to ask another question prematurely and cuts the interviewee off in the middle of his/her train of thought.

This can happen for a number of reasons. The interviewer has:

- questions made out in advance that he or she feels he/she must stick to
- too many questions prepared and tries to get through all of them
- not been confident enough to pick up on the interviewee's point and seek clarity
- not been listening to the interviewee
- focused on the questions and forgotten to hear the gems that came up in the responses
- not been spontaneous and has instead stuck to the prepared questions rather than responding to the information being given
- been evaluating himself/herself as an interviewer while the speaker is talking
- not been concentrating on the message.

A great interviewer is a great listener. They will respond to the interviewee in a spontaneous way and at the same time remember what their objective was when they started the interview.

A good interviewer has an enormous capacity to listen and respond well to a speaker. His body language and tone of voice are clear and direct and at the same time very encouraging. She listens with her eyes, heart and mind. His interviewing skills put interviewees at their ease. She continuously responds to the information that becomes available to her. He asks the questions that are appropriate to the situation. She reflects back and reiterates the feelings expressed and the words spoken. His attitude towards his work and his interviewees is extremely positive and empathetic. Her pace and pause are excellent, giving the listeners and viewers the opportunity to absorb the information.

Listening and hearing

'First seek to understand, then to be understood.'

(Emerson)

We hear the birds singing. We hear the lambs bleating. We hear a barrage of sounds, some of which are pleasing to the ear and some not so pleasing.

Listening is not to be confused with hearing! Listening is not just hearing the words the speaker is saying, it is also tuning in to the tone of voice used, the body language displayed. Good listening is hard work. It seeks to get into the feeling of the speaker in order to listen at a deep level.

Your manner is important in the way you give and receive information; it

Exercises

You will need to listen to a speaker being interviewed on a chat show by a regular interviewer. Comment on the listening skills of both the interviewer and the interviewee. If you were the presenter of the programme, would you have asked any questions that the interviewer didn't ask? Why do you feel that these questions were relevant?

shows how you respond and behave towards others. This is especially important in the listening process. Tone of voice is picked up in this way. Body language is picked up and processed visually. It is not only the words you say, it is also the manner in which you say those words and the behaviour you engage in that underlines the message sent to the receiver.

So, when you listen in an attentive manner, using an appropriate tone of voice and appropriate body language, you show empathy for the person you are listening to, and a productive outcome is very likely for the speaker and the listener.

Your ears *hear* the words, your mind and heart *listen* to the meaning of the words, thereby listening to how the other person feels. True listening requires you to show that:

- you care
- you want to understand
- you are interested in what is being said
- you have an open mind.

You may need to get more information to help find a solution, but you don't interrupt the speaker and you use a tone of voice that is sincere and helpful.

Mark Twain described it perfectly when he wrote: 'Kindness is a language that even the deaf can hear and the blind can see.'

When do you listen best? Is it when you are:
- getting important information?
- getting interesting facts?
- getting directions that need to be followed?
- wanting to learn a new skill?
- wanting to solve a problem?
- wanting to learn the lyrics of a song?
- listening to your favourite music?
- losing yourself in listening to the message?
- being told a story that you find interesting and stimulating?
- in an environment that is conducive to listening?

When do you listen least? Is it when:

- information overload occurs?
- the information is not relevant to your needs?
- you get the wrong vibes from the person speaking to you?
- the speaker's tone of voice is harsh and hostile?
- there is a noise level that drowns out the voice and words of the speaker?
- you don't understand the message?
- you need a break from taking in information?

Not listening!

Not listening can cause a great deal of stress in one's life. Tom, for example, had a listening problem. The fifteen-year-old had a big year ahead of him because he was doing his Junior Cert examination, but he rarely listened to his teachers in class. This annoyed his teachers, especially Ms X, who saw a lot of potential in Tom. When students didn't listen in class she often felt undervalued, having put a big effort into her lesson plans to help them learn. She regularly got annoyed with Tom, in particular, and punished him for his lack of attention.

Tom's listening problem didn't just happen in school. At home his mother was often irritated when he carried on texting while she was trying to talk to him. Sometimes she would punish him by confiscating his phone.

Tom didn't do much better with his homework. He found it hard because he had not been listening in class, but then he made the problem worse by putting on music as he worked, so he wasn't fully focused on his studies. The result was that his homework was rarely done correctly. Not surprisingly, when Tom got his Junior Cert results he was disappointed. What's more, he knew he really could have done better.

Tom is not an unusual case. People often just don't pay attention, or divide their attention between too many things at once.

Exercises

Divide into groups of three, and continue the scripts below as appropriate to each of the situations. Then, using the appropriate voice and body language, speak the dialogue by acting out the two characters. The third person listens and evaluates the different emotions and how they impact on the outcome.

DIALOGUE 1:
Complete this dialogue using the appropriate tone of voice and body language to demonstrate the anger and frustration in Patricia's voice. Imagine how she might feel at the response of her husband James when he dismisses the problem.

'James,' said Patricia, her voice quivering with anger. 'I can't believe you gambled our savings betting on horses, and as a result our children can't get new shoes for the winter.'
'So what?' said James in a harsh, hostile voice.

DIALOGUE 2:
Complete the dialogue using the appropriate tone of voice and body language to demonstrate the disappointment in Mary's voice, and imagine how she might feel as a result of her mother's empathetic response.

Mary bit her lip and her eyes welled up with tears as she told her mother: 'I have failed my exam again.'
'Don't worry, you did your best,' said her mother in a comforting tone.

DIALOGUE 3:

Complete the dialogue using the appropriate tone of voice and body language to demonstrate the hurt and rejection in Pat's voice when his mother dismisses his problem and as a result fails to listen to his concerns.

> 'My friends went to the disco without me,' said Pat.
> 'Get over it,' said his mother unsympathetically.

DIALOGUE 4:

Complete the dialogue using the appropriate tone of voice and body language to demonstrate the disappointment in John's voice, imagining how it makes him feel when his father dismisses the conversation.

'I'm sorry I let you down. I know I shouldn't have failed my exams,'
John said.
'I'm sick of excuses,' said his father.
'You're not listening to me,' John said.
'I am,' said his father, repeating his words.
'You're hearing me, but you're not listening to me,'
John answered.

Now think of examples from your world and examine how you respond to difficult situations in the way you listen, under the following headings.

- Do you hear the emotion being expressed in the tone of voice?
- Do you switch off when you are not interested?
- Do you observe how body language is communicating the message?
- Do you pre-judge the situation?
- Do you dismiss the speaker without giving them a chance to be heard?
- Does your manner allow the speaker the opportunity to be heard?

- Do you allow distractions to get in the way of hearing and observing the intention of the speaker?

Have you ever asked the question, 'Why did you not tell me?' and received the answer, 'I did, but you weren't listening.'

Summary

Listening is a key skill we engage in all our life. We spend much of our waking time listening. Listening is important in all oral communication. You will need good listening skills to take an order from a customer correctly. You will need good listening skills to answer the question you are asked. This is always important, and it is especially important in a job interview as you need to answer the question you are asked, and generally there won't be a second opportunity once the question is answered. More than that, if we develop good listening skills, we learn a great deal from using them.

Listen and learn

L Listening

E Explaining

A Asking

R Responding

N Needing clarification

I Instructing

N Never interrupting

G Generating ideas

SECTION 3
Presentation Skills

Learning Outcomes

Learners will:
- gain an understanding of how to prepare and deliver an oral presentation and answer questions on it
- be able to introduce a speaker
- be able to give constructive feedback.

Introduction

When preparing a presentation, it is important to consider the audience, the purpose of the presentation and how you wish to deliver your message. It might be useful to prioritise your material under the following headings.

- 'Must knows': this is essential information and must be covered.
- 'Should knows': this information often supports the 'must knows'.
- 'Could knows': this could add value and normally supports the 'should knows'.

You need to arrange your material to make it easy for your audience to follow. You must do research in order to have good content. When you know and understand the content, you are able to deliver your message with sincerity and conviction.

Memorable speeches

What makes a speech memorable? There are countless speeches given around the world every day. Examine the following extracts and think about what made them so memorable.

Extract from the inaugural address given by US President John F. Kennedy in 1961:

And so, my fellow Americans: ask not what your country can do for you – ask what you can do for your country.

My fellow citizens of the world: ask not what America will do for you, but what together we can do for the freedom of man.

Finally, whether you are citizens of America or citizens of the world, ask of us the same high standards of strength and sacrifice which we ask of you. With a good conscience our only sure reward, with history the final judge of our deeds, let us go forth to lead the land we love, asking His blessing and His help, but knowing that here on earth God's work must truly be our own.

Extract from the famous 'I Have a Dream' speech given by civil rights leader Martin Luther King in 1963:

I say to you today, my friends, that in spite of the difficulties and frustrations of the moment, I still have a dream. It is a dream deeply rooted in the American dream.

I have a dream that one day this nation will rise up and live out the true meaning of its creed: 'We hold these truths to be self-evident: that all men are created equal.'

I have a dream that one day on the red hills of Georgia the sons of former slaves and the sons of former slave-owners will be able to sit down together at a table of brotherhood.

I have a dream that one day even the state of Mississippi, a desert state, sweltering with the heat of injustice and oppression, will be transformed into an oasis of freedom and justice.

I have a dream that my four children will one day live in a nation where they will not be judged by the colour of their skin but by the content of their character.

I have a dream today.

Extract from Mary Robinson's inaugural address as President of Ireland, 1990:

The Ireland I will be representing is a new Ireland, open, tolerant, inclusive. Many of you who voted for me did so without sharing all my views. This, I believe, is a significant signal of change, a sign, however modest, that we have already passed the threshold to a new, pluralist Ireland ...

May God direct me so that my presidency is one of justice, peace and love. May I have the fortune to preside over an Ireland at a time of exciting transformation when we enter a new Europe where old wounds can be healed, a time when, in the words of Seamus Heaney, 'hope and history rhyme'. May it be a presidency where I, the president, can sing to you, citizens of Ireland, the joyous refrain of the fourteenth-century poet as recalled by W.B. Yeats, 'I am of Ireland ... come dance with me in Ireland.'

Extract from US President Barack Obama's inaugural speech in 2009:

Let it be said by our children's children that when we were tested we refused to let this journey end, that we did not turn back nor did we falter; and with eyes fixed on the horizon and God's grace upon us, we carried forth that great gift of freedom and delivered it safely to future generations.

Thank you. God bless you. And God bless the United States of America.

Extract from the speech by Joe Connolly, captain of the Galway senior hurling team, after winning the All-Ireland Hurling Championship in 1980. The speech was delivered in his native Irish but still resonates with young and old today:

People of Galway, after fifty-seven years the All-Ireland title is back in Galway ... It's wonderful to be from Galway on a day like today. There are people back in Galway with wonder in their hearts, but also we must remember people in England, in America, and around the world, and maybe they are crying at this moment ... People of Galway, we love you!

Delivering a speech

The swan makes swimming look smooth and easy, but it has to paddle hard to give that impression. When giving a presentation you can make it look smooth on the outside, even though you are paddling away underneath. Take comfort from the fact that the audience sees what you present, not necessarily what is going on within.

Audience research

Preparing a speech is like buying a present. In order to buy the most appropriate present you need to know the person's interests, so you can add to what they have already. You also need to package it in the most appropriate way to create a sense of anticipation and surprise.

How many presents bought are never used because the people giving them are just guessing rather than doing their research? By the same token, how many speeches are delivered that go right over the audience's heads because they have little or no relevance to the audience's needs?

So, first of all, learn a little about your audience.

How to introduce a speaker

Introductions are a two-way process, like introducing two people meeting for the first time. In the case of introducing a speaker, it is important to use the same process. You introduce the speaker to the audience and the audience to the speaker. You should also introduce the topic and its relevance to the particular audience. Giving background information on the speaker is also useful; it can add to the audience's understanding and sense of anticipation, and gives the speaker a head start. Like any other speech, your introduction should be researched and rehearsed, and have a beginning, a middle and an end.

EXAMPLES

Suggested introduction of the speaker to the audience for the speech entitled 'Celebration' which follows:

Tonight I'd like to introduce you to Sarah O'Connor. Sarah is our current Divisional Governor and has spent many years participating in the communication and leadership programme. I know many of you know Sarah. For those of you who don't, I believe you too will enjoy listening to her message. The title of her speech is 'Celebration,' in keeping with the birthday celebrations you have helped organise. Ladies and gentlemen, please give a warm welcome to Sarah O'Connor.

As you can see, a well-thought-out introduction with relevant information will help put the speaker at ease and connect the audience with the topic and why it is important and interesting to them.

EXAMPLES

Suggested introduction of the speaker at a fundraising event:

Ladies and gentlemen, it is my pleasure and great honour today to introduce to you a person who has shown courage and conviction in coping with her son's bone marrow transplant. She is now part of a fundraising committee that is gathering money for the leukaemia trust fund. Their aim is to raise €25,000 and she is so grateful to all of you for your contribution that she wants to share her journey and let you know the great cause you are contributing to. Ladies and gentlemen, on your behalf I'd like to invite Pauline McMahon to the podium to share her experience with you.

Speech structure

Putting a structure on a speech is like knitting a jumper: you cast on the stitches (introduction), continue to knit the jumper (body) and cast off the stitches (conclusion). Then you must stitch all the pieces together to make the final garment. Putting the correct structure on a speech is as vital as sewing up the pieces of the jumper properly.

The best speeches have a beginning, a middle and an end (structure), and are relevant to the audience. The delivery is clear and concise.

Tips for making a good speech

1. Keep it simple.
   - Too many choices can cause confusion.
   - Too many words can distort the message.

2. Understand that the spoken word is different from the written word.
   - *Appeal to all their senses*, they are more likely to remember the message.
   - The spoken word must be understood first time because *listening is transient*.
   - *Repetition* may be necessary to underline a point.
   - Don't speak over your audience's heads; this requires that you do *research* as they may know less or more than you.
   - You need to incorporate as many channels as possible to accommodate as many *learning styles* as possible.

3. Remember, your body language and gestures send messages too.
   - Your *gestures* should give the same message as your words.
   - Your *body language* will convince the audience as to your *conviction* on the subject – it is hard to convince others if you are not convinced yourself.
   - You need to show you are *in control*. Walk to the podium with the weight of your body on the back of your heels – this will give you better *posture*.

4. Focus on the message.
   - You should *bond* with your audience in the first minute.

- *Lose yourself* in the message; *focus* your energy on delivering your message in a clear and concise manner.
- *Never evaluate yourself* during the delivery of your speech as it will cause you to lose your spontaneity and as a result you will make mistakes.
- Stick to the *time limits*; it is a useful *discipline* that enables you to condense your thoughts. *Props* can add value, but don't distract the audience by introducing them before they are appropriate.

5. Think about your speaking voice.
   - Your voice is a priceless gift of nature. It is the means by which you communicate. Use it for *maximum effect*.
   - When all is said, it is down to *content* and *delivery*. Arrange the content in the most effective way and deliver it in the most appealing and convincing manner.
   - Speak slowly and *pronounce* your words properly.
   - *Pause* for effect.
   - Be *positive*, be *prepared*.
   - It is not just what you say, but how you say it.

6. Be unique.
   - Don't copy anyone else's style; let your own *personality* shine through.

7. Structure your speech.
   - *Signposts* show us the way. Can you imagine being in a strange part of the country trying to find your way without signposts?
   - Remember to start with the *Introduction*, move on to the *Body* and finish with the *Conclusion*.
   - By following these instructions, you will produce *clear information* that is obvious to the audience.

8. Research your audience.
   - Who are these people?
   - What are their tastes, values and interests?
   - How will what I have to say add value to what they already know?
   - Will it save them time and effort?

9. Have conviction.
    - When one has true conviction about a topic or subject, it is very easy to take ownership of it and present your talk in a clear and concise way. You will convince your audience more by being sincere and genuine yourself.

10. Avoid minimising.
    - You will dilute your message if you use *minimising* language.
    - Avoid language like 'I suppose,' 'it's not important ...'
    - Use 'I believe, I suggest ...' Use body language to enforce your message.

11. Avoid distracting mannerisms and crutch words.
    - Don't fidget or use inappropriate body language – this will dilute your message. Avoid crutch words like 'you know', 'eh', and 'em'.

Celebration Speech

Mr Toastmaster, fellow Toastmasters, friends and guests.

I am very proud and honoured to be present at your Toastmaster club's tenth birthday party to celebrate with you the wonderful communication skills, the bonds of friendship, and the blossoming of so many past and present Toastmasters we have enjoyed over the years. These listening, thinking and speaking skills are so essential if we are to reach our potential as human beings.

The old Chinese proverb comes to mind:
If you want one year's prosperity grow grain
If you want ten years' prosperity grow trees
If you want one hundred years' prosperity grow people.

This Toastmaster club has made an immense contribution to growing people. Tonight you are entitled to look with pride and satisfaction on what you have achieved. Tonight I visit this Toastmaster club in the capacity of Divisional Governor. This role has enabled me to develop

---

my leadership skills. I owe a great debt of gratitude to this club, because it was as a direct result of your efforts that I have had the opportunity to participate in the Toastmasters' programme. This has given me and many others the opportunity to face life's journey with more confidence and better communication skills.

Our great founder, Ralph C. Smedley, said: 'The ability to communicate in a friendly debate before an audience is partly a gift of nature and partly a cultivated art.' In my early days in Toastmasters, I was in awe of Toastmasters who had cultivated the art of effective communication. Thankfully, I too have developed that skill. I have obtained an expanded vision of the role of communicator, and because of the confidence I have gained through Toastmasters I now regard speaking opportunities as stepping stones, not stumbling blocks.

So I would like to thank this Toastmaster's club for introducing me to this wonderful organisation. To the founding members who are present here tonight, I salute you. To the present members, I congratulate you on combining all your skills to stage this wonderful tenth birthday party. Your attitude has certainly been your altitude. I'm sure you will continue the legacy and give many more people the opportunity to develop their communication skills.

Finally, I would like to leave you with a quote from the great Bernard Edmonds: 'To dream anything you want to dream, that's the beauty of the human mind. To do anything you want to do, that's the strength of the human will. To trust yourself to test your limits, that's the courage to succeed.'

May you continue to make your dreams come true.

Questions at the end of a presentation

There are different types of question and each type needs to be handled in a different way. The types of question you are normally asked are: information seeking, clarification seeking, leading questions and questions to which you don't know the answers.

Information-seeking questions

The key to answering information-seeking questions is to be an expert on the subject matter. You must also consider how relevant the answer is to the whole audience. If it is only relevant to one member of the audience, you might consider talking to that person later.

Clarification-seeking questions

It is important to be able to explain further a piece of information if required to do so. You must have a depth of knowledge of your subject.

Leading questions

Leading questions often begin with 'Do you think ...?' If you suspect that someone is out to get you, it is best dealt with by asking, 'Do you have a view on that yourself?'

Questions you don't know the answer to

It is better to admit that you don't know, but do promise to find out and let the person know at a later date.

When taking questions from the floor, it is important to listen to the question and to seek clarification if you don't understand it. Write it down. Repeat the question to make sure each member of the audience has heard it. Answer it in a clear and concise way. Then check whether your reply was adequate to their needs. Invite more questions and finish within the time allocated. Thank the audience for their questions.

Asking questions in an appropriate way

'Curiosity killed the cat and information made him fat' is a well-known saying. It is important to be curious and to be able to ask the right questions, to have shared understanding, better information and mutual support. We also need to ask questions of ourselves to find solutions, to challenge our thinking and to move forward in the most appropriate way. Inventors with enquiring minds have opened up new possibilities for the world. Putting the first man on the moon started with a question: what would it take to put a man on the moon?

Storytelling

People love to hear good stories. They can be a great source of information, inspiration, wisdom and entertainment, and people learn valuable lessons from them. Telling stories is a great attention getter. Good stories reinforce your message and as a result contribute to the overall presentation or speech. Stories linger in the minds of the audience long after the content of the presentation is forgotten.

A story is often used to start or end a presentation, setting a scene at the outset or leaving the audience with a memorable message. In all, storytelling is a very useful medium to help you connect with the audience.

The story of Jack and the Beanstalk – to mention a universal tale – demonstrates that a simple story can be entertaining and full of suspense and that simple dialogue and simple characters can be used to communicate a message. It also demonstrates that a story can have universal appeal and can withstand the test of time when it appeals to the target audience (in this case young children). It does this by incorporating the basic emotions and spirit of adventure that can bring about possible and worthwhile change. It also incorporates many different components of communication in its content.

Folk tales can leave us with a memorable message and the moral of the story can provide us with condensed wisdom by being creative in the use of subject matter to teach a lesson.

Telling a story in a way that appeals to young children can add credibility and excitement.

The story of Jack and the Beanstalk gives us a good template for constructing a personal story. This fairytale has a beginning, middle and end. As there is suspense and anticipation throughout the story, it lends itself to the effective use of pauses. The telling of the story can be enhanced by a storyteller who is aware that effective pause is one of the most potent skills a storyteller can have. It gives the audience the opportunity to assimilate the message and fuels their imagination as to what is going to happen next.

There is a tremendous opportunity to use vocal variety as the characters in the story are so contrasting, and there are a variety of different moods displayed by the characters in the enacting of the story. The play on words is another enhancing element. We expect the giant to have a different vernacular and the introduction of the syllables 'FE, FI, FO, FUM' is an amazing play on words. The introduction of four vowel sounds gives us the opportunity to have a feast of sound in a few syllables. The story lends itself to the imagination and children are kept on the edge of their seats throughout.

The tale presents us with images (visual), through words and sounds (auditory) and through feelings and sensations (kinaesthetic), as well as through smells (olfactory) and tastes (gustatory).

The whole story becomes rich in meaning. We are taken away from a world of destitution and poverty and brought to a world of possibility. The story is told through simple characters and simple dialogue and it gives us the opportunity to use our mind's eye to visualise the different scenes.

The story includes the four primary feelings: mad, sad, glad and scared. It also touches on the spirit of adventure that is part of being human. And, after a lot of scary moments, the story has a happy ending.

Feedback

Being able to give feedback in a friendly, direct and non-threatening way gives the speaker an opportunity to improve.

Constructive criticism gives you the opportunity to rethink how you would do things and gives you food for thought so that you can become more effective in what you do. It recognises the positive aspects of your business/presentation/project and provides the incentive to try even harder to reach the next level by giving you the opportunity to reflect on others' opinions. The ideal way to provide feedback is to give suggestions and examples of how improvements can be made. At the same time, it is vital to acknowledge the strengths of the business/presentation/project.

Feedback given in an appropriate way motivates the speaker to want to improve his or her skills. Evaluation or feedback is generally an opinion and there are as many opinions as there are people. Opinion isn't fact, so it is vital that any feedback is given in such a way that the evaluator separates the speaker from the behaviour and that the evaluator uses language like: 'My opinion is ...,' 'I'd like to suggest ...,' 'You might consider reinforcing your message at the end; I believe it could add value to your already powerful message.'

Exercises:

Go back to the Celebration speech and answer the following questions:

1. Was the speech relevant to the occasion and the audience?
2. Did the speaker acknowledge the input of the audience?
3. Did the speaker show the benefit of the Toastmasters' programme?
4. Did the speaker use strong mental images?
5. Did the speaker uplift the audience?
6. What could the speaker do to improve the content of the speech?

Feedback in the business context

We are often asked for feedback in other circumstances. For example, a business may ask you for feedback so they can ensure they maintain standards or to identify areas they may need to improve. This is also an opportunity for us to offer our opinion. Here is an example of a feedback sheet you might see in a hotel.

The Grand Hotel

We appreciate your feedback!

Please rate your experience with us under the following headings:

	Excellent	Very Good	Good	Fair	Poor
Making your reservation	❏	❏	❏	❏	❏
Check-in	❏	❏	❏	❏	❏
Cleanliness	❏	❏	❏	❏	❏
Friendliness of staff	❏	❏	❏	❏	❏
Bedroom facilities	❏	❏	❏	❏	❏

Presentation in the media

News stories are often presented differently by the national and the local press. For instance, the national press and radio will present a sensitive news story differently from the local press and radio.

Shane Brophy, journalist with *The Nenagh Guardian*, gives us this insight into presentation in national and local media.

'The modern media has developed dramatically over the past twenty years or so.

'Years ago a major incident could take days to come to national attention. Now with the advent of mobile phones, social networking sites and online chat rooms, you could know what has happened at the other side of the world within minutes. News today is immediate.

'It is the very same in an Irish context, but the advent of modern technology has provided new challenges, too, particularly for the local radio and newspaper. Nowadays, the advent of twenty-four-hour news channels and news organisations updating their content by the minute on their websites, is squeezing the options open to local news organisations on how they can present the same story.

'The vast majority of local newspapers in Ireland are published mid-week, so if a story of national interest breaks on the Friday of the previous week, while local journalists would have more time to research and compile their reports, it is likely that the story will have been covered fully by their cousins in the national media.

'From this point of view, it is up to the local reporter to come up with a different perspective when compiling the same information in their report. However, compiling a news story from a local and a national perspective are quite different.

'In a national newspaper context, the bottom line is readership figures and the more dramatic or sensational the story, the more copies of their paper will be lifted from the shelves the following day.

'It is different for local newspapers. While they are always looking to get more people to buy their product, they also have to be sensitive so as to not alienate their existing readership in what is a confined marketplace. The local newspaper has to exist in its local area long after a big story has died away from national prominence.'

Summary

The Ps in Presentation:

- Prepare
- Package
- Pertinent to audience needs
- Participate
- Present
- Perform
- Paint a picture
- Pass on knowledge
- Persuade
- Project your voice
- Pause for effect
- Paraphrase for emphasis
- Personal story.

SECTION 4

Group Discussion and Decision Making

Learning Outcomes

Learners will:

- have the opportunity to participate in group discussion and negotiated decision making
- be able to participate in generating fresh ideas through brainstorming
- understand the process of contributing effectively in formal meetings
- know about the roles and functions of the management committee
- have a better understanding of the different kinds of communication techniques and have the opportunity to practise communication in a formal and informal setting
- have a better understanding of group dynamics and how to contribute effectively in group participation
- be able to have effective conversations and give and receive accurate information.

Negotiation

'Let us never negotiate out of fear,
But let us never fear to negotiate.'

(US President John F. Kennedy's inaugural address, 1961)

Negotiation is a communication process used to work out agreements with people. The best outcome is when it is mutually beneficial to both parties. It often requires a buyer and a seller.

Tips for the successful negotiator

- Work out agreements with people.
- Negotiate – compromise is better than deadlock.
- Know how the negotiation process works.
- Establish a good relationship with the other party.
- Know your own needs and wants, and the reasons for them.
- Know the other person's needs and wants.
- Establish your goal.

We negotiate on a daily basis. For successful negotiation we need planning skills, listening skills, assertiveness skills, empathy skills, communication skills and evaluation skills. We need to be able to break down information and to make a judgement call, to treat the other party with respect, to be able to ask the appropriate questions in a way that is non-threatening. Attributes that are effective in negotiation are trustfulness, respect, creativity and reliability.

EXAMPLE

The following is an example of a potential employee negotiating a salary deal with a potential employer. He is asking for more money than the firm had intended offering. The difference is €5,000. This example shows how the negotiating process works.

Employer: If I were to give you a salary of €45,000, then I would have to increase your target sales figure by an extra €10,000 a month.

Potential Employee: If you were to start by increasing the target sales figure by €5,000 per month it might be more realistic as I will need to establish relationships with your clients and maintain and increase business with them going forward.

Employer: If you agree to increase your sales target by €5,000 for the first three months, we can then review the target figure at that stage with a view to putting it up to €10,000 per month. I can offer you €43,000 at present, and if you reach your targets in three months and take on the extra target I will increase your salary to €45,000.

Potential Employee: I'm happy with that proposal. Will that be built in to my contract?

Employer: Yes, it will.

Potential Employee: I'm happy with that arrangement.

Employer: Great, so when are you ready to start?

Potential Employee: I can start as soon as you need me.

This is a win-win for both parties, which is the ideal outcome.

Successful negotiators work out agreements with people. They aim to achieve a win-win outcome for both parties. This generally happens when both viewpoints and priorities are taken into account and both parties work on common ground to achieve compromise rather than deadlock.

When negotiating:
- Prepare yourself, plan what you want.
- Be clear and realistic about the facts.
- Play devil's advocate – and prepare.
- Listen and check that you understand the other view/position.
- Surrender assumptions.
- Be willing to find creative, fair solutions.

Negotiating power:
- Be present, state your feelings.
- Be prepared to be direct.
- Bring your entire presence to the situation.
- Expect the positive.
- Bring your authority.
- Look for creative solutions.

Exercise

You need to negotiate a better deal on a car you are purchasing from your local dealership. How do you prepare yourself so as to get the best possible outcome?

Brainstorming

Brainstorming is another way of capturing ideas in a non-threatening way. It is a mechanism used to gather all the opinions in the group and it is often surprising how many ideas come from a group of people when each member feels their contribution is valuable and that it is safe to express their opinion.

In a good brainstorming session ideas flow, and the emphasis is on getting people to voice their thoughts in a way that is safe and non-threatening.

The advantages of brainstorming
Brainstorming gives groups the opportunity to generate ideas or find solutions to

problems in a non-threatening way. Judgement is suspended so that all the ideas in the group can be heard, and each idea is considered as valuable as the next.

Would it help your club or organisation to get fresh ideas by brainstorming? If so, you must set out ground rules and make it safe for participants to air their views.

State your topic clearly and simply to start. Let participants know the objective of the exercise and the kind of ideas that are being sought. Ideally the participants should have information in advance as it helps them to have been thinking before they come to the meeting. They know what is expected of them. Limit the number of participants and, to get fresh ideas, invite a few outsiders – this will prevent 'group think' creeping into the session.

Involve the participants, allocate different roles and get one person to act as leader. This person must be fair, impartial and willing to hear all ideas and encourage all participants to say what they think. Encouraging non-verbal communication is also vital in this informal setting and helps all participants to contribute. Another member should act as secretary, jotting down key words.

- All ideas must be recorded and the ideas-generating session should be kept on track.
- No evaluation of ideas should take place while brainstorming session is in progress.
- Limit the time of the session.
- It is quantity not quality that counts at this stage.
- Brainstorming is about creativity, so keep the ideas flowing.
- Welcome diverse ideas.
- Allow participants to build on previous ideas.
- Allow a combination of ideas.

In conclusion, thank everyone for their presence, participation and for generating so many creative ideas. Perhaps you could invite them for a cup of tea and leave a box on the table to accommodate afterthoughts.

A brainstorming session will also provide:
- instant feedback – get to know how the other members of the group are thinking

- an opportunity to use all contacts and talents in the group
- a wealth of knowledge and imagination
- different ideas in a short space of time.

The sky is the limit when you switch on your imagination, but don't get lost in detail when brainstorming.

Mind maps

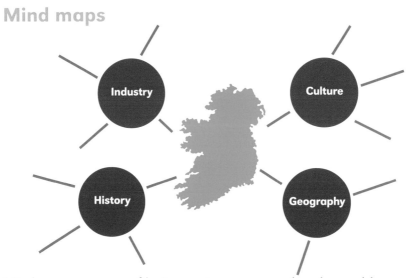

Mind maps are a way of brainstorming your own thoughts, and here you will find that one idea quickly triggers another. In the above example, used in preparation for an essay on 'Ireland Today', the Culture stem could be subdivided into sport, music and literature. Each of these stems can then subdivide and create more thoughts for you to explore. Mind maps provide us with a means of exploring our thoughts and doing something with our ideas (Buzan, 2006).

It's often quite surprising how much we find we know, or remember, about a particular subject when we use mind-mapping to access the recesses of the brain.

Exercise

Generate your own mind map by creating three extra sub-stems to each stem above and continue mind mapping from there.

Formal meetings and management committee skills

Successful meetings are conveniently scheduled, well organised and productive. They start and end on time. The objective of the meeting is clearly stated and the Chairperson works toward the best possible outcome.

Effective meetings

In order for participants to contribute effectively in meetings, it is necessary to have a formal structure, to have a leader who will lead by example and to have the team working towards a common goal. Your role may be different depending on whether you are: Chairperson, Secretary, Treasurer, Public Relations Officer (PRO) or a regular Committee Member. Regardless of the particular role you hold, to contribute effectively in a formal meeting it is necessary to co-operate, to communicate, to respect others and to be accountable and transparent in the manner in which you perform your duties.

Effective meetings are about achieving results, be they information giving, information receiving or problem solving.

- It is imperative that the purpose of the meeting is clearly outlined.
- The agenda is the road map and there should be a clear time limit for each item on the agenda.
- The discussion should be kept on track.
- Each member has the right to be heard. The majority rules but the minority has the right to be heard.
- When a decision is reached, the chair should allocate clear responsibilities depending on the skill mix within the team and also the availability of the team member(s) to contribute to the result.
- It is also important to take turns doing the hard tasks, as this keeps all members feeling motivated, contributing to the task at hand and ultimately to the successful results of the team.
- Meetings should start and finish on time as members' time is valuable. Time management is a discipline that is vital for the successful outcome of meetings.

A management committee's primary function is to manage the resources in the club or organisation. This means looking at the present situation and the requirements

of the club or organisation. Management involves planning, organising, delegating and controlling. The management committee members are involved in the process of setting and achieving short- and long-term goals. Their leadership and motivational skills help the other group members to concentrate on the goals that have been set and keep them focused on achieving them. They cannot hire or fire so they need to be able to guide and inspire.

In order for a team to be effective the following principles must be adhered to.
- Team goals must be clear.
- The roles of both management committee and other team members should be clearly defined.
- All communication should be clear and concise.
- All decision-making procedures should be well defined.
- The behaviour of all group members should benefit the organisation.
- A balanced participation is essential at all times.
- Group rules must be established.
- There must be an awareness of group process at all times.

Leadership and teamwork are vital components of a successful management committee. The Chairperson is responsible for leading the group towards:
- achieving the task – by influencing the direction and pace of the teamwork
- building and maintaining the team – by creating a pleasant and productive climate which makes it easy for members to contribute

- facilitating the team members – by bringing information and ideas to the team and encouraging them to enhance their skills.

All good management committees will assess their progress on a regular basis. They will evaluate their decisions, goals, processes and performances. Using a SWOT analysis one can identify the present position of the club or organisation.

SWOT Analysis	
Strengths (internal)	**W**eaknesses (internal)
Opportunities (external)	**T**hreats (external)

Golden rules of meetings
1. Appoint a Chairperson.
2. Circulate agenda.
3. Arrange items in order of priority.
4. Use an appropriate setting.
5. Have procedures for decisions to be taken.
6. Look at previous meeting decisions.
7. Acknowledge matters arising from minutes.
8. The Chairperson should know the basic rules of procedure, be fair, impartial and help the group accomplish its purpose.
9. Create the right atmosphere.
10. Deal with hidden agendas.
11. Manage the time of the meeting effectively.
12. Review progress and test solutions.
13. Be goal orientated.
14. Minutes should be recorded with individual responsibilities.

Qualities of an effective chairperson

- A good planner.
- A good organiser.
- A good role model.
- Committed.
- Fair.
- A good listener.
- Open-minded.
- A quick thinker.
- Resourceful.
- Able to speak well.
- Able to assimilate information.
- Trustworthy.
- Representative of the group.

Duties of a chairperson

1. To be familiar with the structures and rules of the group.
2. To encourage participation.
3. To be observant at meetings.
4. To deal with conflict.
5. To keep proceedings in order.
6. To keep the discussion on track.
7. To extract ideas and opinions from all members.
8. To maintain order.
9. To make decisions.
10. To lead and encourage the committee to work towards the common goal.
11. To give each member the opportunity to be heard and give their viewpoint.
12. To ensure that planning and evaluation takes place.

Qualities of an effective secretary

- Well organised.
- Good writing skills.
- Concise.
- Able to assimilate information and commit it to paper.
- Tactful.

- Reliable.
- Confidential.
- Maintains good working relationships.

Duties of a secretary
1. To draw up notice of meeting and agenda.
2. To record accurately the minutes of the meeting.
3. To deal with all incoming and outgoing correspondence.
4. To note attendance and apologies.
5. To record decisions.

Qualities of an effective treasurer
- Well organised.
- Accountable.
- Honest.
- Understands financial reports.
- Able to keep a track and trace system in place.

Duties of a treasurer
1. To be transparent and accountable for all incoming and outgoing money on behalf of the club.
2. To be a signatory on the cheque book with at least one of the other officers.
3. To produce an income and expenses account.
4. To have accounts for Annual General Meeting (AGM) independently audited.

Qualities of a regular committee member
- To be committed to the aims of the group.
- To be willing to work as part of the team.
- To be responsible.
- To have time to give to the group.

Duties of a regular member
1. To be familiar with the structures and rules of the group.
2. To prepare for meetings.
3. To participate fully and actively in meetings.

4. To listen and respect other members' views.
5. To encourage other members to participate at meetings.
6. To carry out the tasks allocated to them.

Summary

Different roles require different skills to contribute effectively in formal meetings. However, it is by using the skill mix within the team, to perform the tasks and achieve the best possible results for the team, that each member is motivated to co-operate and contribute their particular talents. It is also important to help all members in the team to grow and develop and to give each willing member the opportunity to participate in different roles as the need arises.

Working in groups

The following are some interesting facts about geese you could use in daily living. (McNeish, 1972)

Facts	Lessons
As each goose flaps its wings when it flies, it creates an 'uplift' for the birds that follow. By flying in a 'V' formation, the whole flock adds 71 per cent greater flying range than if each bird flew alone.	People who share a common direction, purpose and sense of community can get where they are going more quickly and easily because they are travelling on the trust of one another.
When a goose falls out of formation, it suddenly feels the drag and resistance of flying alone. It quickly moves back into formation to take advantage of the bird immediately in front of it.	If we have as much sense as a goose we stay in formation with those headed where we want to go. We are willing to accept their help and give our help to others.

Facts	Lessons
When a lead goose tires, it rotates back into the formation and another goose flies to the point position.	It pays to take turns doing the hard tasks and sharing leadership. As with geese, people are dependent on each other's skills, capabilities and unique arrangements of gifts, ideas, talents and resources.
The geese flying in formation honk to encourage those up front to keep up their speed.	We need to make sure our 'honking' is encouraging. In groups where there is encouragement, production is much greater. The power of encouragement (to stand by one's heart or core values and encourage the heart and core values of others) is the quality of 'honking' we generally seek.
When a goose gets sick, is wounded or shot down, two geese drop out of formation and follow it down to help and protect it. They stay with it until it dies or is able to fly again. Then they launch out with another formation or catch up with the flock.	We should stand by each other in difficult times as well as when times are good.

Applying lessons learned from geese in your classroom or organisation (REST)

Respect each other's contributions towards achieving the common goal.

Encouragement makes it easier for all team members to make a valid contribution through co-operation and collaboration.

Shared leadership gives all members of the team an equal sense of purpose and responsibility. This affords them the opportunity to be effective in a number of different roles.

Time management allows the team to make the best use of time by taking turns doing the hard tasks and co-operating as a team to make the most efficient use of team efforts. It also measures progress towards achieving the result and recognises that time out is important and that team members will need others to support them when times are tough.

Exercise

How can we apply the lessons from geese so that we can contribute to and be effective in group discussions, setting goals and achieving them, while at the same time giving each team member the opportunity to grow and develop their skills?

Group dynamics

People join groups for different reasons. They may want to learn something. They may want to share skills and resources. They may have been asked to join the group to bring expertise and experience that is useful to the group in working towards their goal. They may need to interact socially.

Group dynamics, which are the interactions between members, are often complex and subtle and need to be acknowledged and worked through so that the group can journey through the different stages in group development. Once you know about group dynamics, it will give you confidence to bring the group through the different stages of development, and help you understand what stage your group has reached in group formation.

Stages in group development

In order to be effective in groups it is necessary to understand that groups have four identifiable stages as they grow from infancy to maturity. These stages reflect the process that humans go through as they grow from infancy to maturity: infancy, adolescence, early adulthood, mature adulthood.

The forming (infancy) stage reflects feelings of nervousness, anxiety, excitement, insecurity, wondering ('Will I fit in?'), doubt about whether or not there is enough

time to commit to the task, needing further clarification as to what is expected from the group.

This is the stage where the facilitator needs to inform the group of the overall task and the overall objectives. The facilitator needs to listen to the concerns and address these concerns in a fair and impartial way. A group task can be a good way of breaking down barriers and sharing information. It may also give the group a sense of belonging and a realisation that each member has clues that are pertinent to solving the problem. This also helps to build trust and empathy.

The next stage is the storming (adolescence) stage, when the group gels together. The facilitator can help the group to work through this process by allowing members to voice their fears and concerns.

It is essential that differences are acknowledged and respected and that conflict is worked through in a way that identifies what the problems or perceived problems are. Solutions, and an agreed way of working that is acceptable to all members, are then found. This can be a good time to draw up a group contract so that each individual, and then the group, is clear about what is expected of them. The fact that each member helps to formulate these rules gives a sense of ownership and responsibility.

The next stage is the norming (early adulthood) stage. There are now ground rules in place. Members have the opportunity to have any concerns dealt with in a way that reassures them that they have a contribution to make to the group.

The members are now settling in to the task at hand and are prepared to listen and evaluate the contribution of others. They are also becoming aware that by using all the skills in the group in the most appropriate way, they are most likely to achieve the best possible outcome.

The next stage is the performance (adulthood) stage. There is a productive and pleasant atmosphere prevailing. The focus is now on delivering the best possible results. There is commitment and a sense of satisfaction as the members encourage one another to work through the process.

The positive energy of wanting the best outcome is converting into a great performance by the team members. There is a strong sense of 'we are doing it together' and a recognition of the contribution made by all members to achieving the results (Tuckman, 1965).

A good attitude makes a positive contribution. The process of contributing effectively in group settings and in formal meetings requires a number of skills and attributes: goal setting, leadership, teamwork, sharing, monitoring, co-operating, respect, communication, listening, evaluating and being able to celebrate successes and achievements. The process will be enhanced by participants who have an excellent attitude.

Exercise

Look back at Berne's TA model in Section 1. How will participants' attitudes affect the productivity of the group and the outcome from meetings?

Summary

There are many methods of participating in group discussion and negotiated decision making. Understanding the stages in group development is important to the outcome of the group – it gives the facilitator the confidence to work through the process in order to achieve the goal and at the same time maintain the team.

Good group work happens when there is a good leader who will lead by example. It happens when there is a common goal, co-operation, good communication skills, and when members respect each other and there is a monitoring system in place. The group works towards the best result and when they achieve it they celebrate their success, which often motivates them to set an even more challenging goal.

Conversing and taking messages

Conversation is an important part of life. It is a means of connecting with our family, our work colleagues, our friends and people we come across in our daily lives. There are many occasions when we have formal conversations. These could be described as 'conversations with a purpose', for example negotiating a loan or doing a job interview.

Conversation

The art of good conversation lies in using oral skills, listening skills, tone of voice and body language in the most appropriate way to ensure that your message is communicated well. The receiver then has the opportunity to respond, either by asking an appropriate question or making a relevant comment. It is a two-way flow and requires mutual respect and sincerity.

Conversations can be informal or formal depending on their nature. An informal conversation is generally spontaneous and does not have a desired outcome in advance. Job interviews, on the other hand, are an example of a conversation with a purpose. The interviewer wants to get the best applicant to match the job requirements. The interviewee wants to demonstrate how he/she matches the needs of the employer.

An interview with a bank manager to negotiate a loan would also be a conversation with a purpose. The bank manager needs to know that you are a suitable person to lend money to, that you have the repayment capacity to service the loan (based on your salary and commitments), and that you look at the most suitable repayment term to service the loan. The interviewee, on the other hand, wants to get the best value for money in order to keep costs down.

Each day of our lives we are likely to have several conversations, ranging from chit chat and casual conversations to conversations that inform, advise, extract information, give instructions and seal deals.

In our casual conversations we are natural, spontaneous and empathetic; we are at ease and have the freedom to be ourselves. We can lose ourselves in the conversation and enjoy interacting with another person.

Formal conversation, on the other hand, often causes people stress because they are concentrating on the outcome rather than delivering the message in the most appropriate way. Effective formal conversation requires preparation and anticipation to give the participant the opportunity to be able to think and speak logically under pressure. Good listening skills are essential, as well as the use of pauses, sincere and open body language, an appropriate tone of voice and the ability to condense your thoughts so that your message is clear and concise. It is also important to answer the question that you are asked and avoid going off on a tangent. As the spoken word is fleeting, it is important to speak slowly and articulate and enunciate your words clearly, so that none of your message is lost.

Silence can be very hard to handle when it happens during a conversation, whether a formal or informal one. It can feel as if communication has just broken down. For the inexperienced speaker, this can be embarrassing, even terrifying. The worst thing to do, of course, is to panic – then your message really will be lost in delivery.

Silence and pauses are natural moments in every exchange. They give people time to reflect on what they've heard, or consider what they are going to say. And, yes, sometimes we run out of things to say – or maybe we've simply said enough!

It's important to remain calm during quiet moments in a conversation. Don't feel under pressure; in fact, taking a moment to pause can be very effective. Breathe evenly and realise that being calm and quiet can add to your presentation.

What makes conversations effective?

- Start with a little small talk.
- Listen with sincerity.
- Look the speaker in the eye, show that you are listening.
- Don't look impatient for the speaker to finish speaking.
- Don't cut them off mid-way through a sentence – it can be intimidating.
- Share the conversation.
- Listen and pick up on points made.
- Ask questions to clarify what the speaker means.
- Don't pretend to understand if you do not.
- Don't belittle the speaker with any of your responses.

- Don't be afraid of pauses – they give the speaker and listener the opportunity to consider their responses.
- Share your experience with the listener only if it is relevant.
- Don't go off on a tangent.
- Don't be put off by their accent or speaking voice – listen to understand.

Telephone conversations/message taking

The telephone is often the first point of contact with potential customers, so it is important to make sure that there is a standard response and that the telephone is answered in a courteous and efficient manner. It is also important that every message is directed to the appropriate person and that messages are taken accurately. Every call must be dealt with and calls must be returned to the caller when necessary.

Message pad for taking messages

Important
message

For

From

Time   **Date**

Phone

❑ **URGENT!**

Message

Telephone conversation

1. Establish rapport.

   Receptionist: Good morning, ADK Bank, Helen speaking.

   JS: Good morning, Helen, may I speak to Marian Jones?

   Receptionist: Who's calling, please?

   JS: Julie Simpson.

2. Clarify the purpose of the call.

   Receptionist: What is it in connection with?

   JS: It is in connection with an investment that is due to mature next week.

   Receptionist: Is she expecting your call?

   JS: I wrote to her last week and told her I would be calling.

   Receptionist: OK, I'll put you through.

   JS: Thanks.

3. Communicate clearly.

    Receptionist: I'm afraid she is not available to take your call at present. She is speaking to a client.

    JS: That's OK. When would be a good time to call her back?

    Receptionist: If you wish, I'll have her call you back as soon as she finishes with the customer.

    JS: That would be great. How soon can I expect the call?

    Receptionist: Within the next hour.

    JS: I'll be at home until 11.30 a.m.

4. Listen actively and close the call.

    Receptionist: Can I have your telephone number?

    JS: Certainly, 0678888222.

    Receptionist: That is 0678888222.

    JS: That's it.

    Receptionist: Great, thanks. You'll hear from us within the hour. Bye for now.

Listening and hearing are, of course, very important in the message-taking and message-giving process. The attitude and the ego state of the receiver of the call will determine their manner and tone of voice and hence the way they interact with the caller.

When callers like what they hear, they are more likely to feel comfortable giving you information. This happens when a trust relationship is built up and the listening process is worked through (including any clarification necessary), ensuring a positive outcome. This is achieved by effective listening, excellent attitude and assertive behaviour when dealing with each caller.

Adult to adult is the only appropriate behaviour in a business situation.

First impressions last!

Whatever the reason for the telephone call, you will never get a second chance to make a positive first impression. You may well be the first point of contact with a potential customer, so it is vital that you come across as professional and helpful. Ideally you should answer the phone after two or three rings. You are the medium of the company's message.

'The true spirit of conversation consists in building on another man's observation, not overturning it.'

(Edward Bulwer-Lytton)

Exercise

In pairs, demonstrate effective message taking and receiving. One person is booking a holiday. The other person is a travel agent giving them all the details over the phone. Make sure all the information is given clearly, and recorded appropriately by the other person.

Summary

Conversation and message taking are about speaking and listening, asking the appropriate questions and clarifying the information if there is any doubt. They are also about testing the transfer to ensure that the message sent is the message received.

Preparing for Job Interviews

Learning Outcomes

Learners will:

- be able to examine job descriptions and identify the requirements for the post
- be able to anticipate interview questions and prepare responses
- be able to prepare a CV and cover letter and relate their experience to the job on offer.

Introduction

The objective of a job interview is to find the most suitable person to match the job requirement and to fit in with the ethos of the organisation. You will need to know the job specification and prepare your best examples to demonstrate that you match what the company wants. It is also important to be in the right frame of mind and to be courteous and polite. You cannot prepare for all eventualities, but if you examine the job requirements, most questions can be anticipated and you can match the skills that are appropriate to the job on offer. You will acquire confidence from knowing that you have prepared as thoroughly as you can.

Remember, most interviewers like interviewees who are assertive and will tell you that they hire for attitude, so it is worth cultivating a good attitude.

What is a job interview?

An interview is a sales meeting, where you have the opportunity to sell your skills, strengths and experience to a company or organisation which needs those abilities.

You need to bring out your best self by identifying your skills, strengths and experience, and show that these are particularly applicable to the job on offer.

The best way to identify the requirements of the job is to examine the job description. You will have thought out in advance how you can demonstrate your suitability, and will show this by giving examples from your previous work experience, school or leisure interests.

It is necessary to prepare and refine your answers so that the sales opportunity is fully availed of, and that by the end of the interview the interviewers are fully aware that you can meet the job requirements. By refining and developing your answers in advance, you will make the best use of the time given in the interview.

You have already learned that there are a number of media through which we perceive how another person is communicating their message. Therefore, it is imperative that you are aware that the interviewer is evaluating you through the auditory, the visual and the kinaesthetic modes. Your words, body language and tone of voice must all send a convincing message.

The interviewers will be evaluating:

- how they see you (visual)
- how they hear you (auditory)
- how they react to you (kinaesthetic).

Now that you know that an interview is a sales meeting, it is important to identify your skills, strengths and experience and convert them into benefits for the job on offer.

1. Before you enter the interview room, think of your greatest achievement. Your body language will benefit from this positive thought and you will

walk with an air of confidence. Keep the weight of your body on your heels as this will give you extra gravitas.

2. Shake hands with the interviewers when you enter the room. It is a good way to begin, connecting with the interviewers with your handshake as well as with your verbal greeting. It is important to have a good firm handshake as this shows confidence and respect. A limp handshake can be a reflection of someone who is unsure of themselves; this may send the message that you lack confidence and are uncomfortable around people. Too firm a handshake can send the message that you are overpowering.

3. Do not sit down until you are invited to do so. If the interviewer forgets, you can ask politely: 'May I sit down?' Sit comfortably. Listen to one question at a time and try to answer it in a way that demonstrates that you are a good fit for each task on the job description. Where possible, start your answer using the same words as they used in asking the question, for example: 'Why are you interested in this job?' 'I am interested in this job because …'; 'What have you to offer this company?' 'I believe I have a lot to offer this company, such as …' Pause to collect your thoughts. Effective pauses are important throughout the interview as they give you a chance to construct your next sentence and they give the interviewers the opportunity to assimilate the information you have given them.

4. Avoid fidgeting – this will distract the interviewers from what you are saying. Look at the person speaking to you and to whom you are replying. This means making eye contact. Occasionally, glance at the other interviewers during your reply.

5. At the end of the interview, you may be asked if there is anything you would like to add. This question presents you with a number of opportunities. First, to show courtesy by thanking the interviewers for inviting you to the interview. Second, there is an opportunity to raise something that has not come up in the interview and is relevant to the job on offer. Third, there is also an opportunity to go back to a question that you feel you did not answer sufficiently and to add value to your previous answer.

6. Finally, there is an opportunity to ask a question. It might be as simple as 'How soon can I expect a result from today's interview?' Then there is the opportunity to close the sale: 'I would like to confirm my interest in this position …'

7. Remember to leave as positively as you arrived.

The importance of being prepared

- Know where the interview is being held.
- Arrive in good time.
- Know the job requirements.
- Bring supporting documents with you if required (certificates, references, etc.).
- Match the need with the want by thinking out your best example which will demonstrate that you have that particular skill.
- Think before you speak and try to avoid any crutch words that might distract from your answer.
- Learn about the organisation – this can be done by visiting the organisation and looking at their website.
- Anticipate questions and prepare responses.
- Concentrate on delivering the message.
- Be aware of your body language.

The whole package

It is the whole package that counts: appearance, words, body language and tone of voice make up the whole package.

As you never get a second chance to make a first impression, it is important that you send the right message as soon as you enter the room – your body is communicating through your posture, eye contact, smile, gesture, voice and touch. Dress code should be in keeping with the organisation you are being interviewed for. A general rule of thumb is dress sensibly, smartly, wear neutral colours and be really well groomed.

> **Casting the die:** You cast the die in the very first answer, therefore it is vital that you are thoroughly prepared to communicate an appropriate answer, keeping it relevant to the job on offer.

Making the conversion

A forward is expected to convert good possession into scores because without scores the match can't be won. Similarly, an interviewee is expected to convert skills and experience into a benefit for the job on offer, and is therefore more likely to win the job as a result.

During the interview

- Concentrate on delivering the message that you are an excellent match for the job description.
- Listen to one question at a time, don't try to anticipate what question is coming next; you can only deal with one at a time.
- Your voice is the medium of your message; use it to best effect.
- Never evaluate yourself during the interview; you will lose your spontaneity.
- Answer your questions in a clear and concise way.
- Sit comfortably and avoid fidgeting or distracting mannerisms.
- Use eye contact with the person speaking to you.
- Use the language of conviction; if you are not convinced, it is hard to convince others.
- Be honest.
- Use the opportunity at the end of the interview to ask a question or provide more information on something that will add value.
- Be courteous – thank the interviewers for the invitation to the interview.
- Close the sale.

Sample Interview Marking Sheet used by members of an interview panel

Interview Marking Sheet					
Interview date:		Job title:			
Time	Name	Capacity to meet the needs of the job	Communications	Enthusiasm	Knowledge of the job/CV	Total marks
		/40	/20	/20	/20	/100

Interview panel

Print name:_____   Print name:_____   Print name:_____

Signature:_____   Signature:_____   Signature:_____

Interview questions

Here are the different types of questions you may be asked in an interview.

- Open questions
  'Tell me about yourself' is often used as the first question in an interview.
- Closed questions
  Did you enjoy the course? Probing single facts. Yes/No answer with a couple of reasons for your answer.
- Probing questions
  'Why did you change your career?' Checking information.
- Reflective questions
  'You feel you can handle difficult customers well?' Problem solving.
- Leading questions
  'You wouldn't mind working overtime, would you?'
- Multiple questions
  'Tell me about a time when you had to make a difficult decision. How did you evaluate whether you made the right decision or not?' These questions test your ability to make good judgements.

Competency-based interviews

Apart from technical knowledge and ability, employers may have a list of competencies or criteria they are looking for specifically. The following is a list of competencies often sought by employers.

- Communication: information giving, information receiving, listening, interacting and problem solving.
- Teamwork: co-operating, sharing, using the skill-mix in the most appropriate way to achieve the goal.
- Results orientated: setting goals that are relevant and achievable.
- Responsibility: being consistent and dependable in carrying out your daily duties.
- Problem solving: being able to deal with problems in a calm and professional manner.
- Customer care: giving all customers a professional and courteous service.
- Decision making: being able to make clear and objective decisions, gathering the necessary information and then making an informed decision.
- Assertiveness: being able to make your point heard, calmly and clearly, without becoming aggressive or disrespectful.
- Adaptability: being able to adapt to the situation and use your skills to bring about the best possible result.
- Resilience: being able to do the hard tasks as well as the ones that are easy or the ones you enjoy.
- Empathy: being able to see the situation from the other person's viewpoint and working through any obstacles to ensure the best outcome.
- Motivation: being a naturally motivated person, able to work through challenges, helps to motivate others and ensures more positive outcomes.
- Building relationships: being able to get on with people from different cultures, different ages and different backgrounds is an important attribute.

Even if you have been out of the workforce for a number of years, you may still have developed these competencies through involvement in local communities, teams/groups and committees, or through personal development.

How can you demonstrate that you have these competencies? Think of examples from school, work, voluntary organisations, individual and team sports and other challenges you had to overcome to succeed at something you found difficult. There may be many examples from your personal life as well as from your school or professional life.

Exercise

This particular situation, involving job descriptions, requires action. How will you resolve it?

The manager has given his secretary three job descriptions for three different posts that he wants filled as soon as possible. He has instructed three interviewers to meet, and to devise an appropriate set of questions based on the job requirements.

The job descriptions are for a Hotel Receptionist/Clerical Officer, Shop Manager and a Home Care Co-ordinator.

A new recruit to the organisation, who thought the job descriptions were to be scrapped, tore them up into small pieces and put them in the bin. There are no other records and the manager is not contactable. You need to reconstruct the material to give a copy to the interviewers so they can prepare their interview questions. Each job description has ten points. The problem is, you don't know which points relate to which job.

Your task is to reconstruct the three job descriptions.

Divide up into groups of three. Read through the following list of job points and think about the role they might apply to. Reconstruct the pieces based on those jobs' roles. Construct three job descriptions, giving an accurate account of the requirements in each so that the interviewers can construct their questions based on these job descriptions.

Now match the appropriate points to the correct job.

JOB POINTS

1. Good office and administration skills, and a high level of PC competency.
2. Work as part of the overall team, passing on information to the appropriate person and co-operate with each member in the team to provide an excellent service.
3. Become familiar with the requirements of the Dept of Health and make sure these rules are understood by the carers.
4. Organise and prioritise work to meet deadlines.
5. Take full responsibility for the shop's accounting procedures. Take full responsibility for balancing cash takings each day and lodge each day's takings in the night safe each evening.
6. Promote the benefits of doing business with the hotel and communicate with the manager to ensure that customer service issues are identified and resolved.
7. Deal with a wide range of people from different backgrounds on a daily basis, communicating in a clear, courteous and concise manner.
8. Deal with queries, booking and feedback.
9. Ensure that the window displays are changed regularly and that they are appropriate to yearly celebrations and events.
10. Accurately file all documents so that they can be tracked and traced when necessary.
11. Comply with all health and safety requirements, policies and procedures.
12. Overall management and development of the shop, working to an agreed work plan and target set by the owner.
13. Ensure the shop is kept clean and tidy at all times.
14. Responsible for the inventory and security of all equipment and fittings on the premises.
15. Have a background in the caring profession.
16. Maintain a productive and pleasant working environment, where staff work as a team to provide excellent customer care service and good public relations.
17. Ensure that all checks and controls are in place to deliver a quality service.
18. Be a self starter and a problem solver.
19. Have good communication and empathy skills. Be able to give clear instructions and get feedback from the carers and the families. Introduce the Home Care Service to newly referred clients and families.
20. Maintain a safe working environment and be familiar with health

and safety requirements so that nobody's safety is compromised.

21. Be able to lead and manage the team to achieve the best outcome for the clients.
22. Recruit, train and appraise all staff of their expected duties, and have checks and controls in place to ensure a quality standard of work.
23. Answer the telephone in the appropriate manner.
24. Be able to make informed decisions.
25. Follow cash handling and till procedures to ensure till out-turns.
26. Ensure that health and safety statement is read, understood and signed off by all carers.
27. Ensure confidentially at all times.
28. Responsible for the proper inventory and accounting of all incoming goods.
29. Have good administration skills.
30. Be familiar with report writing, scheduling/staff rosters and managing petty cash.

Hotel Receptionist/Clerical Officer: This role requires a highly motivated person who loves dealing with people. This person must be thorough and organised and be relied upon as an excellent front-line person. He/she must have excellent administration and office skills as well as a high level of PC competency. He/she will be required to listen and co-operate with the other team members to ensure a quality service is delivered. He/she must be vigilant in selling the benefits of the business at all times. He/she must operate within health and safety guidelines.

Job Description:

1.
2.
3.
4.
5.
6.
7.
8.
9.
10.

Shop Manager: This role requires a responsible person with at least three years' management experience in a similar role. He/she must be familiar with recruiting and training staff and preparing staff rotas, be able to manage staff to ensure that customer care is evident and that they are maximising on sales opportunities. He/she must be familiar with accounting procedures and inventory procedures and used to working to targets to increase turnover in the shop. He/she must also be familiar with shop layouts and window dressing.

Job Description:

1.
2.
3.
4.
5.
6.
7.
8.
9.
10.

Home Care Co-ordinator: This role requires an energetic person who comes from a caring background. He/she will need to be able to work in a team setting and will need to be a good decision maker. He/she will need to possess excellent communication skills as well as listening and problem-solving skills. He/she will require good administration skills.

Job Description:

1.
2.
3.
4.
5.
6.
7.
8.
9.
10.

In the reconstruction of these job descriptions, what have you learned about preparing for an interview? Write down your findings and discuss them.

The following is a list of questions that might be asked at interview for each of these jobs. Practise expressing your answers.

Possible questions for Hotel Receptionist/Clerical Officer position

1. What do you know about the hotel?
2. Explanation of the job.
3. CV walk through and questions.
4. Work experience – level of responsibility, best part of job, worst part of job – what did you learn from the work?
5. What are your strengths and weaknesses?
6. How do you organise your work on a daily basis to meet deadlines?
7. What level of PC competency do you have?
8. How do you manage stress at work?
9. If every possible job were open to you, which one would you like the best?
10. What do you consider your greatest achievement?
11. How would you ensure that the service we offer to our customers is second to none?
12. Do you prefer to work on your own or as part of a team?
13. What makes a team successful?
14. What are your hobbies?
15. How do you think people who know you would describe you?
16. What qualities do you have which make you suitable for this job?
17. Is there anything you would like to ask or add?

Possible questions for Shop Manager's position

1. You have worked in a number of different shops. What have you learned from these?
2. Tell me about a time when you had to deal with a difficult customer.
3. What kind of management style do you like best?
4. How do you organise your work on a daily basis to meet deadlines?
5. Do you work to targets?
6. How do you know that you achieve a high standard?
7. How would you like to be managed?
8. How would you motivate staff to give their best?
9. How would you ensure that we offer our customers an excellent service?
10. Have you ever dealt with a customer on the telephone who was unhappy with the service provided?
11. Tell me about a person you would not like to work with.
12. How would your colleagues describe you?
13. Have you ever had the opportunity to re-organise your job, or make any suggestions for improvements?
14. How does your supervisor know that you do your job properly?
15. How would you supervise your staff?
16. Tell me about a project you took through from beginning to end.
17. How do you feel about doing repetitive work?
18. How would you maintain, grow and manage sales?
19. What is the most difficult aspect of managing people, sales and resources?
20. What kind of experience have you had of staff rosters?
21. What checks and controls would you put in place to ensure that a track and trace system ensured total transparency?
22. Why should we give you the job?
23. Is there anything you would like to ask or add?

Possible questions for Home Care Co-ordinator position

1. Please give an outline of your CV to date detailing the aspects that are appropriate to the position.
2. Can you give some examples of working on your own initiative in a work environment?
3. Do you prefer to work alone or as part of a team?
4. Tell me about two different roles you played in a team.
5. What experience have you in the following areas: report writing, staff rosters?
6. Tell me about a time when you had to decide between two or three courses of action. How did you make your decision? How did you evaluate whether you made the right decision or not?
7. How would you introduce the service to a newly referred client?
8. How would you like to be managed?
9. What do you think are the most important personal attributes needed to work with people who need care?
10. What is the most difficult aspect of caring for people?
11. Tell me about a person you would find it difficult to work with.
12. How would you manage a care worker who frequently arrives late to work?
13. How would you develop and ensure a well motivated staff?
14. What differentiates you from the other candidates?
15. Is there anything that you would like to ask or anything you would like to add?

Curriculum vitae

Curriculum vitae (CV) preparation is a vital part of job-seeking. A CV is a sales document. It should be easy to read, clear and well presented. Where possible it should do its job in a maximum of two pages. When compiling a CV ensure there are no spelling or grammar errors, do not lie and make sure there are no gaps in time.

Your CV has two objectives:

1. To secure an interview by quickly showing that you fulfil the job requirements as described in the job advertisement.
2. To act as a prompt for the interviewer by providing the details that back up your claim to be the ideal candidate for the job.

CV layout

Personal Details: At the beginning of the document, include your name, address, contact number(s) and email address if you have one. It is not necessary to include your age/date of birth, marital status or nationality.

Personal Profile: A short profile of your background and the skills you have to offer is very effective as an introduction to the CV.

Educational History: In reverse chronological order (starting with the most recent), include the schools and third-level institutions you have attended, the dates and the courses of study.

Employment History: In reverse chronological order, detail your past employment. Each job should include dates, name and address of employer, position held, and your responsibilities. The list of responsibilities should be kept clear, concise and to the point.

Further Training: Include any training you have done outside of school or college, for example ECDL, first aid, manual handling, etc. You must include the dates and the name and address of where you completed the training.

Hobbies and Interests: Include any hobbies or interests you may have, however unimportant you may feel they are. It is critical not to include hobbies or pursuits that you are not actually interested in! This section of your CV is often used by the interviewer to 'break the ice' or to calm your nerves. You must be able to chat about your hobbies and interests.

Voluntary Work: This is an important section that is often overlooked when preparing a CV. Include any work that you do not get paid for, however small.

Examples include charity fundraising, under-age hurling coach, member of local Tidy Towns group, committee member, residents' association and parents' association. This voluntary work demonstrates that you are enthusiastic and willing to get involved in extracurricular activities. It also shows that you are committed, hardworking and willing to work as part of a team to achieve a common goal.

Achievements: Include any relevant achievements/prizes you have been awarded. They do not have to be strictly work-related. Achieving a county medal in hurling or football, for example, shows that you are goal orientated and can work as part of a team. Being captain of a team would also show that you have leadership ability. Do not include certificates you have received for training. These should go in the Further Training section.

Additional Information: If you have any additional information you feel is relevant to the job on offer, you should include it here. Otherwise, you can leave this section out. If you have a car/driver's licence you can include it in this section.

Referees: You must include two referees. These should include a previous employer or an educational reference. Always ask for permission before you include someone's name on your CV.

The following are examples of two CVs, the first for a foreman with experience in the construction industry, the second for a person experienced in manufacturing and retail.

Joseph Bloggs
Main St, Ballyshannon
Co. Westmeath
Tel: (093) 900000
Mob: (087) 0000000
email: joebloggs@mail.com

PROFILE

An experienced foreman with excellent communication and people skills. A strong team player, leader and motivator who works well with others. Energetic, organised, determined and versatile.

EMPLOYMENT HISTORY

June 2000–March 2011: Ballyshannon Construction, Ballyshannon, Co. Westmeath

Position: Section Foreman

Responsibilities: • Planned work for construction gangs
                    • Ordered materials
                    • Ensured all employees had a Safe Pass and were suitably trained
                    • Carried out inspections on machinery to ensure it was in working order
                    • Liaised with company directors and subcontractors
                    • Organised permits
                    • Adhered to Health and Safety standards

EDUCATIONAL HISTORY

1997–2000:   Athlone Institute of Technology, Athlone, Co. Westmeath
              Diploma in Construction Management (2.1)

1992–1997:   Ballyshannon Vocational School, Ballyshannon, Co. Westmeath
              Completed the Leaving Certificate

FURTHER TRAINING

In-house training at Ballyshannon Construction

2010:   First Aid

2009:   Safe Pass

2009:   Safety Management

2006:   Manual Handling

HOBBIES AND INTERESTS

- GAA, walking, darts
- Member of Ballyshannon GAA Club

ADDITIONAL INFORMATION

- Full clean driving licence
- Car owner

REFEREES

Mike O'Meara	David O'Brien
CEO	Engineering Lecturer
Ballyshannon Construction	Athlone Institute of Technology
Ballyshannon	Athlone
Co. Westmeath	Co. Westmeath
Tel: (093) 111000	Tel: (093) 222000

Mary Smith

33 Parkmore

Clonmore

Co. Offaly

Tel: 087 0000000

email: marysmith@mail.com

PROFILE

A quality-focused individual with many years' experience in manufacturing and retail. Committed to meeting deadlines. A helpful and flexible team player, organised and dependable.

EMPLOYMENT HISTORY

2006–2011:	Medmore, Tullamore, Co. Offaly
Position:	Manufacturing Team Member
Responsibilities:	• Worked as part of a team assembling products
	• Conducting daily and monthly batch sampling quality tests
	• Trained new employees in assembly skills

2002–2006:	Dolan's Newsagents, Clonmore, Co. Offaly
Position:	Shop Assistant
Responsibilities:	• Provided excellent customer service
	• Handled cash and cards
	• Ordered stock
	• Displayed and organised stock
	• Cleaned the premises daily

1985–2002:	SynPackaging Ltd, Tallaght, Co. Dublin
Position:	General Operative
Responsibilities:	• Worked in packaging department and operated as a machinist

1980–1985:   Clonmore College, Clonmore, Co. Offaly
              Successfully completed the Leaving Certificate

FURTHER TRAINING

2008:   Medmore in-house training
              • First Aid and Defibrillator
              • Manual Handling
              • Chemical Handling
              • Health and Safety
2007:   Offaly Training Centre, Tullamore, Co. Offaly
              ECDL

INTERESTS AND ACTIVITIES

Reading, walking and going to the cinema.

VOLUNTARY WORK

2008–present: Parkmore Residents' Committee, Clonmore, Co. Offaly
Responsibilities: • Maintaining housing estate
              • Maintenance of green area, planting of trees and flowers
              • Liaising with County Council
              • Attending residents' committee meetings

REFEREES

Available on request.

Letter writing

Well-chosen words in well-written letters produce results.

A letter of application accompanying your CV has the following objectives:
- To introduce you to the employer and show your interest in becoming part of the organisation.
- To create a positive picture of you as a capable person.
- To encourage the receiver to read your CV.
- To get you an interview.

Before you begin to write:
- Check you have the correct name and job title of the person you are writing to.
- Know something about the business – what they do, make, sell, etc.
- Know what you want to say.
- Know the order in which you want to say it.
- Then write a draft of the letter.

Ask yourself:
- Why am I writing this letter?
- What am I trying to achieve?
- How do I think the reader will react?
- If you are not happy, write it again.

Letter details:
- Use the advertisement.
- Underline or write out the words the employer uses to describe the type of person they want for the job.
- Look up these words and use others of the same meaning in your letter.
- Write good, positive things about yourself – no bad information.

● Tell them what you can do and what you will bring to the organisation.

With a suitable CV and covering letter in place, you should be confident applying for any job that matches your skill set.

Exercise

The following are five job advertisements. Choose one that may be suitable to you and complete a CV and letter of application.

Shop Assistant required for busy Newsagents. Previous experience not necessary as full training will be given. Must be of neat appearance, have friendly manner and be prepared to work on Saturdays. Apply in writing to Ms Helen Moran, Moran's Newsagents, 101 Main Street, Portlaoise, Co. Laois.

DEPOT MANAGER – The successful candidate will be fully responsible for the management of the depot and will report directly to the Group Sales Director.

Duties will include: Management of the day-to-day functions of the business, managing and growing established customer base, generating new business through targeted and innovative selling, addressing customer product queries and service liaison.

Requirements: Excellent computer skills, ability to motivate and manage your team, target/deadline focused, ability to work on own initiative, excellent organisational, communication and interpersonal skills.

Application is by CV and covering letter to PR Kelly Ltd, Castle House, Kilmallock, Co. Limerick.

SALES REPRESENTATIVES REQUIRED

We have five new positions for Sales Executives nationwide. The role requires calling in on industrial, commercial and private clients to establish which services are required and to sell those services. The successful applicants will receive a basic salary, and will also receive commission for reaching set targets. Leadership qualities are desirable and promotion is possible for individuals with these qualities. A self-starter is preferred. The successful candidate will also be willing to learn. You will be adaptable and hard-working and will want to progress through the company. A full-time permanent position will be made available to those successfully completing a trial period. Apply with CV and covering letter to ABC Sales, Main Street, Gorey, Co. Wexford.

APPRENTICE ELECTRICIANS

We have vacancies for 1st, 2nd and 3rd year apprentice electricians for industrial and commercial contracts. First-year applicants must have passed Leaving Certificate and existing FÁS registered candidates must have industrial and commercial experience.
Own transport is essential.
Apply with CV to Electrical Contracts Manager.

Nurse's Aids – Nationwide

Full-time Nurse's Aids required to look after patients in hospitals/nursing homes. Duties to include washing, bathroom duties, feeding, etc. Minimum of one year's hospital-based experience required. For people without the required level of experience, we have a two-week pre-employment course.

Please email CV and cover letter to nurses@mail.com or by post to ABC Medical, Main Street, Bettystown, Co. Meath.

The following is an example of a suitable letter of application for the first job advertisement above. The key components are listed: **1** Sender's address; **2** Recipient's name and address; **3** Date; **4** Subject line; **5** Salutation; **6** Introductory paragraph; **7**, **8** Further paragraphs; **9** Concluding paragraph; **10** Closing; **11** Signature and typed name of sender.

1. 33 Parkmore
    Clonmore
    Co. Offaly

2. Ms Helen Moran
    Moran's Newsagents
    101 Main Street
    Portlaoise
    Co. Laois

3. 26 June 2011

4. Re: Shop Assistant Position

5. Dear Ms Moran

6. I would like to apply for the job advertised in the *Leinster Express* on 22 June.

7. As you will see from my CV, I have previously worked in a newsagents and have experience dealing with customers, handling cash and stock control. I have excellent communication and people skills.

8. I am quite prepared to work on Saturdays.

9. Should you require any further information please do not hesitate to contact me. I look forward to hearing from you in the near future.

10. Yours sincerely

11. _____
    Mary Smith

For those completing the FETAC Work Experience module, here is a sample of a suitable letter when applying for work experience.

33 Parkmore
Clonmore
Co. Cork

Ms Kate Kennedy
Meadowlark Nursing Home
Millstreet
Co. Cork

27 April 2011

Re: Work Experience Placement

Dear Ms Kennedy

My name is Pauline McEvoy and I am currently completing the FETAC Level 5 Healthcare Support Award. The aim of this award is to give learners a qualification that they can use to find employment in the healthcare sector, mainly as care assistants.

I believe I have the skills and qualities required to work as a care assistant. I am hard-working, reliable and flexible. I have excellent people skills and I am a team player.

One of the modules I have to complete as part of the Healthcare Support Award is Work Experience. It is a requirement that I complete a work placement in a nursing home.

I would be most grateful if I could meet with you to discuss the possibility of completing my work experience at Meadowlark Nursing Home. I will telephone you in the coming days to arrange a meeting with you.

Should you require any further information please contact me at 087 0000000.

Yours sincerely

_____

Pauline McEvoy

A–Z of Interviews

A is for Attitude/Assertiveness/Adding value.

B is for Behaviour/Body language.

C is for Compatibility/Commitment/Closing/CV and Covering letter.

D is for Demonstrating understanding of the job and relating your experience to the job on offer. D is also for appropriate Dress.

E is for Empathy/Effective pause. And for Enthusiasm.

F is for Focus/First impressions.

G is for Greetings, showing Genuine interest.

H is for Helpful (and Honest).

I is for the Image we project to the interviewers.

J is for Joining the organisation, what benefits are you bringing?/ Job Description.

K is for Keeping alert/Knowledge.

L is for Listening to one question at a time.

M is for Making the interview count.

N is for being Natural, showing your genuine self.

O is for the Opportunity to make the right impression.

P is for Preparation/Pace.

Q is for Quality assured.

R is for taking Responsibility and for quantifying Results you have achieved.

S is for making every question a Sales opportunity/Specific.

T is for Thanking the interviewers for the invitation to the interview.

U is for Unique selling point, what differentiates you from other competitors.

V is for the Value you bring to the organisation.

W is for Words, using them in a clear and concise way, and for Well presented.

X is for XOB, thinking outside the box.

Y is for You, your ability to work with other team members.

Z is for Zest, showing genuine interest in the job.

MAIN LEARNING OUTCOMES

Learners will be able to:

- gather information from a range of sources
- evaluate information critically and objectively
- apply a reading approach appropriate to the purpose and the nature of the text
- plan and undertake research into a topic using a variety of sources, both primary and secondary
- follow the conventions of writing for a specific purpose (for example business documents, personal writing) and observe the current conventions of written English in relation to grammar and punctuation.

Unit 2

Reading and Writing

Research Methods

Learning Outcomes

Learners will:

- understand the difference between secondary research and primary research
- list the sources of secondary research
- understand reading strategies and techniques for evaluating material
- explain the two types of primary research – qualitative and quantitative
- outline the methods of quantitative and qualitative research
- understand how a questionnaire is designed and the different elements it should contain
- explain focus groups and briefly explain how they are facilitated
- outline other methods of research such as observation.

Introduction

The structured report (covered later in this unit) is an important part of the communications module. To be able to undertake writing the report, it is necessary to understand how research is gathered and carried out. This section deals solely with research methods. To reiterate the learning outcomes, at the end of this section students should be able to explain the difference between secondary and primary research. Students should also be able to distinguish between quantitative and qualitative research.

Types of research

Research can be categorised into secondary research and primary research. Secondary research deals with facts and figures that have already been collected. In a workplace situation, this research can be obtained from either internal or external sources. Primary research gathers new information from interviews, surveys, observations, etc.

Secondary research

As already mentioned, secondary research explores facts and figures that have already been collected. This research has been carried out by another person or body and the findings of the research have already been compiled and summarised. The data that was gathered can be beneficial for other research. There are two main sources of secondary research for the organisation or body that requires this information: internal sources and external sources.

When gathering research, the first step should be to look for internal records within the organisation itself. This information is readily available and should be utilised as it is cheap and less time-consuming to find. Internal research can be gathered from the following sources:

- sales reports and customer records
- financial reports
- personnel reports
- company policies and procedures
- minutes of meetings
- company/organisation databases
- any other reports or research on the company or organisation
- customer suggestion box.

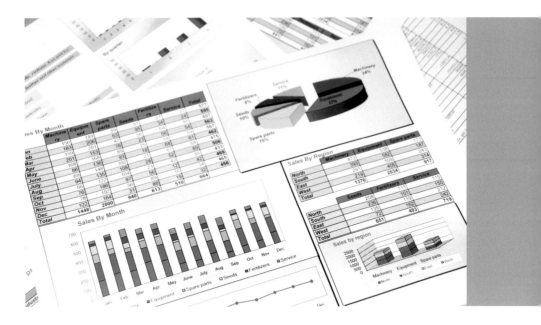

External sources of research

The following are examples of external sources of secondary research. These consist of a diverse range of government bodies, research institutes and corporations:

- government departments
- state agencies (e.g. FÁS and Enterprise Ireland)
- universities
- research institutes (e.g. ESRI)
- marketing research companies
- journals and articles
- OECD (Organisation for Economic Cooperation and Development) reports
- published research reports
- books
- libraries
- world wide web.

Problems with secondary research

Secondary research is not an optimal source of information for the following reasons.

- The research may have been done for another reason, and therefore may not be relevant.
- It may be out of date.

- In the case of facts, errors may have been made in the analysis of the original data.
- The data may not be reliable.
- The research may be biased.

Reading strategies

When undertaking secondary research, you may choose to use information from books, journals, newspaper articles, etc. Here are some reading strategies to help you plough through all that research.

Skimming: getting the general idea of a text without reading every word. This technique is useful if you are reading many different books or journals.

Scanning: used to find out precise information. This reading strategy is used if you are looking for specific details on a topic.

Detailed Reading: this strategy is used when very detailed understanding is needed. When using this technique, highlight relevant chunks of text and make comments on Post-its stuck to the relevant page. Longer texts will require you to take detailed notes; this aids remembering and understanding.

Revision Reading: reading rapidly over text that you are familiar with. At this stage you would try to summarise the material into the main points needed for your research.

Before reading any books, journals, etc. do the following.
- Read the title of the book.
- Read the table of contents of the book.
- Go through the book and look only at the main headings and sub-headings, and any diagrams, graphs or tables.
- Read the summaries at the end of each chapter, and also any review questions.
- Read the introductions and conclusions.
- Finally, read the first sentence of every paragraph.

This technique will allow you to pick out the relevant parts of the book, journal or article and then you can begin reading in more detail, highlighting and taking notes as you go. Once you have finished reading, summarise the information that you have read. Next we will look at how to evaluate the research.

Evaluating the research

Before deciding to use secondary research in, for example, the short report, the following factors should be taken into account.

- Does this research help to answer the research question, or, in the case of the report, does the research help the investigation or provide the information specified in the terms of reference?
- Is the data relevant to the population/organisation/place being investigated? Can the findings of the research be verified by some other source?
- If the research is relevant, verifiable and pertinent to the terms of reference, you should check the age of the data itself – is it out of date?
- Sometimes research questions or investigations might differ but the same data may be used. In this case it may be useful to find out if the same data can be used to answer the investigation. Is the original data available?

If any of the above criteria cannot be satisfied, the data or research material cannot be used. However, if the research material proves useful, it can be greatly advantageous. First, it will save a lot of time and money. Second, it can be a great way of recognising gaps in the current research and it may prompt the researcher with primary research ideas.

Primary research

As valuable as secondary research can be, it often fails to supply all of the answers. Even if relevant data has been found, it may still have gaps. In this case, primary data needs to be gathered. Data can be gathered from surveys, observations, interviews or experiments. It is very unlikely that an observation or experiment will be carried out to gather data for the short structured report that you will be undertaking as part of the communications module. It is more likely that data will be collected by means of a survey or interview for this project.

When primary research is mentioned, two other topics, and their relative merits, often come up in discussion. Have you guessed them? Well, the two topics are quantitative research and qualitative research. Without reading on, you should already have some idea of how to distinguish between these two types of primary research by focusing on the words: quantity and quality.

Quantity refers to a number, or an amount that can be measured. Therefore quantitative research refers to research that can be quantified or measured and listed in statistical form. Surveys or questionnaires are often used in quantitative research. The data gathered can be input into software programs that will convert the raw data into useful statistics.

Quality refers to how good something is. When shopping for clothes the customer may want the clothes to be of good quality. Businesses nowadays are focused on quality assurance, which involves monitoring a product or service and ensuring that certain standards are met. In qualitative research the amount of research is not as important as in quantitative research. Samples tend to be small in this type of research as the emphasis is on the quality of the research itself. Qualitative research involves researching attitudes and feelings, things that can't be really quantified or measured. Interviews and focus groups are examples of qualitative research.

We will now look at the primary methods of collecting data, focusing on both quantitative and qualitative research.

The survey

The survey is one of the most common methods of identifying trends in customer satisfaction ratings. Trends are measured by a technique known as statistical analysis. Interviews and questionnaires are examples of surveys.

The most common reasons for surveys are to:

- measure overall customer satisfaction
- measure a customer's satisfaction with a product/service
- measure customers' satisfaction on delivery times
- measure returns and exchange process satisfaction
- conduct market research on new products or services (Heyman, 2004)
- examine habits within a demographic group.

Telephone surveys

The interviewer interviews the respondent over the telephone. This type of survey can result in some 'hang-ups'. This may be because the respondent had a previous experience where the survey took too long to complete or the questions were hard to understand. If undertaking a telephone survey, keep the questionnaire as short as possible. This type of survey is easily administered and cost-effective, but the sample population is confined to participants with telephones.

Postal surveys

Surveys are sent by post to respondents. This type of survey is self-administered, which has the advantage of eliminating interviewer bias. However, the lack of an interviewer to clarify questions can also be a disadvantage if the respondent is uncertain about what is being asked. This type of survey allows the respondent to be anonymous as he or she does not have to put their name on the questionnaire. Response rates from this type of survey tend to be poor.

Email surveys

Surveys are sent in batches electronically over the internet. The respondent keys in the answers and sends back a reply. The advantages of email surveys is that they have low transmission and collection costs. The surveys can be sent instantly and replies can be very fast. However, response rates can be low. Email surveys often have poorer results than postal surveys. One of the reasons for this is that when the email is sent back it will have the respondent's name attached. The following are recommendations to increase response rates.

- Use *personalised salutations* to make the respondents feel special.
- Use a *link to another web page* containing the survey instead of an email attachment. Then, when the respondents are finished, they can click a button to submit the survey, thus reassuring them that they will remain anonymous.
- *Target the sample population* as they will be interested in the topic and are more likely to send back the survey.
- Respondents will reply quicker if there is an *incentive* for doing so (Michaelidou and Dibb, 2006).

The questionnaire

A questionnaire is a set of questions designed to generate the data necessary to accomplish the objectives of the research project (McDaniel and Gates, 2001). It is a method of data collection and can be administered as part of any of the surveys discussed.

Questionnaires are also used in structured interviews. In a structured interview, the interviewer will ask every interviewee the same set of questions. The success or failure of a survey or structured interview will depend on the design of the questionnaire. Think back to the last time you were asked to fill out a questionnaire – it may have been in the middle of the street in the freezing cold! You may have even told the interviewer that you did not have time to fill it out.

There are many things you need to take into account when designing a questionnaire. It needs to be short and very quick to fill out. If you are considering using this method of data collection for the short structured report, you should think about administering the questionnaires yourself rather than leaving them at different locations, such as reception desks and shop counters, in the hope that someone will fill them out. Also, if the questionnaire contains many opinion questions that require the respondents to think, it may be more useful to carry out an actual interview.

A characteristic of the questionnaire is that it produces data that is comparable. This is because when administering a questionnaire all of the respondents are asked the exact same questions, either by the person distributing the questionnaire, or by going through it themselves. Therefore, the data can be quantified, and so it is a method of quantitative research.

What defines a good questionnaire?

- It will answer the questions outlined in the terms of reference. McDaniel and Gates (2001) recommend that management should be consulted about the questionnaire and sign off on it before it is distributed. For the short structured report your tutor will be the manager! Either way, make sure the questionnaire is satisfactory before being distributed.
- It is estimated that 50 per cent of all people asked to complete surveys refuse to participate. This is because of bad experiences with long-winded question-naires that were difficult to understand. Another reason is giving the question-naire to a respondent who is not part of the sample population. For example, if the questionnaire was designed specifically to investigate the overall satisfaction of students who took part in the Business Studies course, administering the questionnaire to somebody who did a course on Engineering is a waste of time. That student is not part of the sample population. The sample population are students who studied Business Studies. This reason aside, the student is also not interested in the questionnaire topic. McDaniel and Gates (2001) recommend that a questionnaire should be designed only for the intended respondents. A simple screening question at the beginning of the questionnaire is useful ('Are you a student on the Business Studies course? Yes or No').
- Finally, the data from the questionnaire should be easily processed.

Designing a questionnaire

The following is the Ambrose and Anstey (2007) recommended model for designing questionnaires. There are seven elements in this model. Every questionnaire should attempt to include all seven elements.

1. **Demographics**
   Demographics are characteristics of a population. Examples of demographic information are age, sex, income, education and occupation.

2. **Behaviours**

   Behaviours are about people's or organisations' actions. An example of a behaviour question is, 'How often do you shop in Tesco?' Based on the respondent's answer, it is possible to determine the relationship the respondent has with Tesco.

3. **Attitudes**

   This involves assessing the respondent's attitude to a product, service, organisation, etc. This type of question is used to determine the respondent's level of like or dislike, or the respondent's opinion. They are known as scalar questions. These should be used to determine the respondent's attitude, for example:

   The Business Studies course in this institution provides students with the skills and knowledge required for industry.

Strongly Agree	Agree	No Opinion	Disagree	Strongly Disagree
❏	❏	❏	❏	❏

4. **Knowledge**

   A question may be used to assess the customer's knowledge of products, services and organisations. Here are two examples:

   What do you think are the main functions of product X?
   What is the recommended maximum intake of units of alcohol per week?

5. **Predispositions**

   Predispositions are thinking patterns individuals adhere to based on past behaviour. For example, if somebody has a predisposition to be pessimistic the chances are they will be pessimistic towards new ideas. This question evaluates respondents' reactions to change and it should be formatted similarly to a question on attitudes. The example given in the model is as follows:

   How important is the relocation of the Bank of Ireland to your continued relationship with the bank (on a scale of one to six)?

6. **Propositional or Conditional**

   This type of question is designed to assess the conditions that would have to be in place for a customer to change – for example, what reasons would a customer give for changing from one electricity provider to another? One person's reason might be that the competitor claims to be cheaper, another might be that one company is friendlier to the environment. Another example of this type of question would be to assess the reasons why the respondent would change their health insurance provider, for example. If a company or organisation wishes to find out the main reasons why consumers will switch, this type of question is very important.

7. **Intentions**

   Questions attempting to assess the respondent's future intentions cannot provide exact answers, but they can explore the respondent's expected behaviour in the next period of time. Example:

   What is the likelihood that you will change your car insurance provider next year?

It should be noted that a question can satisfy more than one element of the model.

The questionnaire design process

1. Determine the reason for the research. In the case of the short structured report, the reasons will be contained in the terms of reference.

2. Decide the method for administering the questionnaire; is it to be face-to-face, telephone, internet, etc?

3. Choose the types of question to be included. There are three main types of question: closed-ended, scale response questions and open-ended.

   a. Closed-Ended Questions
      This type of question has a limited number of answers to choose from. It involves ticking a box, or circling a category. These questions eliminate interviewer bias because there is no room for misinterpretation of the answer. Closed-ended questions are easily converted into statistics.

i. Dichotomous Questions

These are questions that have two possible answers to choose from. Usually 'Yes/No' or 'Agree/Disagree'. Example:

Are you Male ❏   or Female ❏

ii. Multiple Choice Questions

These questions have a number of alternative answers. When using multiple choice questions it is important to be aware that there may be more alternative answers to the question being asked. This is why a check box for 'other' is useful, and a space for the interviewer to write down the alternative. Example:

What is your occupation?
Farmer ❏   Construction Worker ❏
Teacher ❏   Nurse ❏

The questionnaire designer in this case did not include a space for other occupations not mentioned in the question. Therefore if the respondent does not fall into any of the above occupations, the question will have no response. This is how the question should look:

What is your occupation?
Farmer ❏   Construction Worker ❏   Teacher ❏
Nurse ❏   Other ❏
If other please specify: _____

Make sure that the list of alternatives is not too long. There are two reasons for this: first, the respondent may get confused; second, the respondent may get bored and just tick any of the boxes. This may result in bias because the respondent may tick a box closer to the top of the list. Note that the above question is also an example of a question that includes a demographic element.

b. Scaled Response Questions

These questions are usually used to gauge levels of agreement or levels of satisfaction. They are usually associated with questions that measure attitudes. This is the example we have seen already:

The Business Studies course in this institution provides students with the skills and knowledge required for industry.
Strongly Agree ❑   Agree ❑   No Opinion ❑
Disagree ❑   Strongly Disagree ❑

These questions are also closed-ended questions because the respondent has to choose from the list of alternatives given. This is another example of scaled responses:

The technical support provided by this company is excellent.
1 ❑   2 ❑   3 ❑   4 ❑   5 ❑

In this type of question the interviewer would have to specify what the range 1 to 5 means. In this case it is the same as the above example (1 means strongly agree, and 5 means strongly disagree).

c. Open-Ended Questions

These are questions that provide the respondent with the opportunity to give his or her opinion or provide suggestions. The respondent then replies in his or her own words. The information provided by open-ended questions can be rich in nature. Example:

Have you any suggestions on how we can improve our service?

Open-ended questions can provide more alternatives than closed-ended questions. However, the use of this type of question should be limited. Too many of these questions can extend the amount of time it takes to complete the questionnaire. The interviewer may miss out on some of the points made by the respondent. Also, the answers are hard to quantify. One way of analysing the data in open-ended questions is to give each response a code. As the questionnaires are being analysed, some responses may be the same, and in that case the data can be converted into statistics. Last, open-ended questions are more beneficial when there is an interviewer administering the questionnaire because the interviewer can probe the respondent about his or her answers.

4. Decide on the wording of questions.
    The wording of questions needs to be clear and the questions themselves cannot be biased. Questions phrased in a positive way may result in a positive response; likewise, questions phrased in a negative way may result in a negative response. Example:

    Were you happy with the excellent service that you received in ABC Ltd?

    Appropriate wording must be used to get accurate answers from respondents. Each question should address one topic only and the respondent must understand what is being asked. If the question is unclear it won't be responded to. Finally, the questions should be designed in such a way that the respondent is willing to answer. A respondent will sometimes know the answer to a question but may not wish to share the information. This occurs when questions are of a sensitive nature (e.g. questions on borrowing money and income). A way of avoiding this is not to ask the questions directly of the respondent but to phrase the questions so that they refer to people in general.

5. Layout of the questionnaire.

    a. The first question should be a screening question. This type of question rules out any respondents that the questionnaire does not relate to. For example, if the questionnaire is geared towards students on a specific course, the first question should find out if they are actually on the course. If they are not, it is pointless continuing.
    b. You do not want to discourage the respondent, so the easier questions should come first. Include as many multiple choice questions as possible. Next in line should be scaled questions. If the questionnaire has

open-ended questions, leave them towards the end.

c. A lot of questionnaires finish up with a question containing a demographic element, for example to determine the age group the respondent falls into.

6. Evaluate the questionnaire. Take out unnecessary questions, or edit questions that are too long-winded.

7. If approval is needed before the questionnaire can be distributed, get it at this point.

8. Carry out a pilot survey if possible and make any revisions that are necessary. This involves running a test survey to establish how effective the questionnaire is for meeting the research objectives (McDaniel and Gates, 2001). The feedback received from the pilot survey will help to fix most problems. It will also help to eliminate any technical terms that cause confusion, while questions that are difficult to understand can be edited (Hopewell, 2008).

It cannot be emphasised enough that the questionnaire must be consistent with the objectives of the research or report being carried out. This is the first step in the design process.

Decide how many respondents are needed as a representative sample. This involves determining the sample size. Where a list of respondents is not available, one can be purchased from a reputable panel company which has the right cross-section of respondents. For the short structured report, twenty or thirty respondents would be enough.

Where possible use closed-ended questions. Open-ended questions are harder to analyse. The questionnaire needs to be short, simple and focused on the objectives of the research. Ideally it should take five minutes to fill out, and definitely not more than ten (Hopewell, 2008).

EXAMPLE

The following questionnaire will be analysed to show the different types of question and illustrate how the elements of Ambrose and Anstey's model are incorporated.

Questionnaire on Tourism to St Petersburg, Russia

1. What is your main reason for going to St Petersburg?
   - ❏ a. Business
   - ❏ b. Visiting friends and family
   - ❏ c. Leisure

   This is an example of a closed-ended multiple choice question.
   It establishes the behaviour of the respondent.

2. What sources do you rely on for information about St Petersburg?
   - ❏ a. Newspaper
   - ❏ b. Magazine (please specify)
   - ❏ c. TV programme
   - ❏ d. Internet advertisement
   - ❏ e. TV advertisement
   - ❏ f. Guide books (please specify)
   - ❏ g. Other books (please specify)
   - ❏ h. Brochures of tour operators
   - ❏ i. Word of mouth

   This is another closed-ended multiple-choice question. It provides information
   for the St Petersburg tourist groups on the most useful method of advertising.

3. What deterrents, if any, might prevent you from travelling to St Petersburg?

   _____

   This is an open-ended question. The question contains a conditional element.

4. How would you prefer to arrange your trip?
   - ❏ a. Independently
   - ❏ b. Through your job/studies
   - ❏ c. Tour operator
   - ❏ d. Internet

   This is a closed-ended question that includes an attitude element. It also
   has a predisposition element because the answer will probably be based
   on customers' previous experience.

5. Would you like to travel to St Petersburg with other people who share your interests?

❑ Yes ❑ No

This is a closed-ended dichotomous question. It has the predisposition element as the person will have travelled with or without other people before. It also has the intention element as it outlines future intentions.

6. Are any of these prime considerations in your trip?
   ❑ a. Museums and galleries
   ❑ b. Architecture and monuments
   ❑ c. Theatre
   ❑ d. Customs
   ❑ e. Religion
   ❑ f. Music
   ❑ g. Politics
   ❑ h. Unique shopping
   ❑ i. Photography
   ❑ j. Literature
   ❑ k. Festivals

This is a closed-ended question, but the respondent may tick more than one box. This question includes a knowledge element as it assesses the respondent's knowledge of the area.

7. Please consider the importance to you of these attractions:
   Rate: 1 = must visit; 2 = might visit; 3 = won't visit; 4 = don't know;
   5 = never heard
   [ ] a. St Petersburg city bus tour
   [ ] b. Hermitage Museum
   [ ] c. White Nights festival
   [ ] d. Dostoyevsky Museum
   [ ] e. Pushkin Museum
   [ ] f. Anna Akhmatova Museum
   [ ] g. Mariinsky Theatre (Kirov Ballet)
   [ ] h. Russian Museum
   [ ] i. Peterhof fountains

☐ j. Traditional Russian cuisine restaurants
     (blini with caviar)

☐ k. Peter and Paul Fortress

☐ l. St Isaac's Cathedral

This is an example of a scaled-response question and it also measures attitudes.

8. Are there any other things you would like to do in St Petersburg?

☐ Yes

☐ No

This is a dichotomous question with an open-ended element. If the respondent answers 'Yes', there should be a space left underneath the question for the respondent to add a comment. This is to cover the possibility that not all attractions were mentioned in questions 6 and 7.

9. Do you speak Russian?

☐ Yes   ☐ No   ☐ A little

This is a closed-ended question. It also has a knowledge element.

10. When would you prefer to travel to St Petersburg?

☐ Summer   ☐ Winter

This is a closed-ended dichotomous question. It has a behaviour element and it could also be argued that it has a predisposition element.

11. How would you characterise your job status?

☐ a. Higher managerial, administrative or professional

☐ b. Junior managerial

☐ c. Skilled worker

☐ d. Self-employed

☐ e. Student

☐ f. Pensioner

☐ g. Unemployed

This is a closed-ended multiple-choice question with a demographic element included.

12. To what age group do you belong?

☐ 15–18   ☐ 25–34   ☐ 45–54   ☐ 65 and over

☐ 19–24   ☐ 35–44   ☐ 55–64

This is a closed-ended multiple choice question with a demographic element included.

13. Please enter any other comments you would like to make.

```


```

This is an open-ended question. Open-ended questions are usually used to find out the respondents' attitudes and feelings towards something.

Thank you for taking the time to complete this questionnaire.
(http://www.stanwardine.com/russiansurvey.htm)

Qualitative research

This type of research was introduced at the beginning of the chapter. We are now going to look at it in more detail and also at two qualitative methods of research: focus groups and interviews. We will also mention observation and experiment.

As already stated, qualitative research cannot usually be quantified as it is used to examine attitudes, motivations and feelings. Smaller sample sizes are used here so that in-depth discussions can be held to ascertain people's attitudes and feelings towards a product, organisation or company, etc. Because samples are small, qualitative research may not be representative of the total sample population. Also, the research is very subjective as it is reliant on the interpretation of the researcher. Where possible, qualitative research should be used to enrich results from any quantitative research that was carried out.

Focus groups

The purpose of the focus group is to hold an in-depth discussion on a topic to find out the participants' attitudes and feelings about the subject. This involves holding an in-depth discussion with between eight and twelve participants. The group is led by a person called a 'moderator'. The moderator is not an interviewer. His/her job is to facilitate the discussion. As the discussion develops, more of the participants will be encouraged to get involved.

How to facilitate a focus group

It is unlikely that you will be conducting a focus group for the structured report. Interpreting the attitudes and feelings of participants requires a highly skilled and experienced researcher, not to mention the facilities required to host a focus group. Nonetheless, we will now discuss briefly how a focus group is conducted.

1. The venue should be a conference room or a room that is similarly equipped, with a one-way mirror or video conferencing facility, which allows the researchers and note-takers to view the discussion. Microphones should also be placed in the room in areas where they won't be noticed.

2. The participants should be picked at random from the sample population. Participants from the sample population will satisfy the criteria required for the discussion. The discussion does not usually last much more than an hour and a half.

3. The role of the moderator can be equated with that of the chairperson of a meeting. It is his/her responsibility to ensure that the discussion does not wander away from the topic. A chairperson is required to stick to the agenda of a meeting and the moderator does the same. The moderator must also ensure that everybody gets their say. A problem with focus groups is that one or two people can dominate the discussion, making the discussion less fruitful. The moderator should have good listening and speaking skills, and be able to interpret non-verbal communication. He or she should have good organisation and interpersonal skills. The success of the focus group depends on the skills and experience of the moderator.

4. The focus group will have a discussion guide, similar in purpose to the agenda of a meeting. As already mentioned, it is the moderator's responsibility to ensure that all topics are discussed.

5. At the end of the focus group the moderator may decide to give his/her reaction to the focus group and how he/she interpreted the feelings, attitudes and motivations of participants. However, this is an initial reaction and the moderator may change his/her views once the discussion is seen and heard again (McDaniel and Gates, 2001).

Interviews

There are two types of interview used in research, the in-depth interview and the structured interview. The in-depth interview is unstructured and does not contain a fixed set of questions. In this case the interviewer needs to be highly skilled. The progress of the interview will be based on the participant's answers. Each answer will result in the interviewer asking another question based on the previous answer or asking the participant to elaborate. As it takes a skilled and experienced interviewer to carry out this type of research, it is not a recommended research method for the short structured report.

If you choose an interview as your method of research, it is recommended that you carry out a structured interview. The structured interview is a type of survey, using a questionnaire which can be designed following the guidelines already set out in this chapter. The benefit of doing a structured interview is that all of the interviewees will be asked the same set of questions and the data gathered will be easier to analyse as it is comparable. Guidelines for analysing questionnaires are discussed in the next chapter.

Observation

Carrying out an observation involves researching the actions and behaviours of people by watching what they do. This technique is used in situations where a questionnaire or interview would not be sufficient. The reason for this is that most people are not aware of their behaviour. Take for example your shopping habits in the supermarket. Do you have a certain routine for shopping? Which side do you start at? Would you know exactly the path you took? Chances are you follow this route without thinking, so in cases like this it is better if the researcher carries out an observation and simply watches people doing their shopping. Another example would be observing the most common lunches chosen in the school canteen. It is unlikely that you will carry out this type of research for your report.

Experiment

In an experiment the researcher changes one or more variables – price, packaging, design, shelf space, advertising theme or advertising expenditures – while observing the effects of these changes on another variable (Linehan and Cadogan, 2003). Confectionery companies, for example, might test-market a new product and decide whether or not to continue with that product depending on the result. An experiment is not an appropriate method of research for the short structured report.

Summary

So which is better, quantitative or qualitative research? This is a question researchers have been debating for years. Both types of research have their own set of advantages and disadvantages. Value can be added to research by integrating qualitative and quantitative methods. Both types can be combined, even in a single study. As well as that, a more systematic approach can be taken to qualitative research or a more observational approach to survey research, as this can help to bridge the gap between the two methods. Researchers may decide, for example, to hold a focus group or hold a set of in-depth interviews first and then test the findings by doing a survey to validate the research. Similarly, researchers may decide to do qualitative research to better understand the findings of a survey. When the research being carried out is of great importance, the benefits of investing time and money in both quantitative and qualitative methods far outweigh the costs (Shah and Corley, 2006).

Exercises

1. What are the main sources for secondary research?
2. Explain two reading strategies.
3. Summarise in your own words how a piece of secondary research should be evaluated.
4. What is the difference between quantitative and qualitative research?
5. List three reasons why a survey might be carried out.
6. List and briefly explain the seven elements of Ambrose and Anstey's model for designing questionnaires.
7. In your own words, summarise the questionnaire design process.
8. In groups of four or five, design a questionnaire to examine overall satisfaction with the student shop/canteen.
9. Explain one method of qualitative research.
10. In your opinion, which is better, quantitative or qualitative research?

SECTION 2
The Report

Learning Outcomes

Learners will:
- understand how a report is structured
- understand how questionnaires and interview results are analysed
- understand the correct method of presenting findings
- understand how conclusions and recommendations are formulated.

Introduction

A report may be undertaken for many different reasons. For example, the manager of an organisation may want somebody to produce a sales report for the last six months; or the person responsible for health and safety may be asked to undertake a report to see if the health and safety policies and procedures are up to the standard required. Reports are produced all the time for government departments. There are many different types of report but this text will cover the short structured report.

The short structured report

The short structured report is broken down into the following parts:

- Title
- Terms of Reference
- Method of Procedure
- Findings
- Conclusions
- Recommendations.

Title

This should be short and state exactly what the report will focus on, for example: 'Report on Levels of Customer Satisfaction in JKL Ltd'.

Terms of reference

This section of the report should state why the report was carried out, i.e. the reason for the report. The wording of the terms of reference is determined by the type of report being written. If the main purpose of the report is to provide information the terms of reference would be worded as follows: 'As requested by _____, to provide information on _____.' Sometimes report writers are also asked to make some recommendations. In this case the wording of the report would be as follows: 'As requested by _____, to investigate levels of customer satisfaction in JKL Ltd and to make any necessary recommendations.'

Method of procedure

In this section the author should state how the report was carried out. All methods used to gather the information presented in the findings should be listed here. There are usually three main sources of information: the organisation, secondary research and primary research. Examples of these are outlined briefly here. Further detail is provided in the section on research methods.

Examples of an organisation's internal records:

- company policies and procedures
- company accounts
- records of meetings

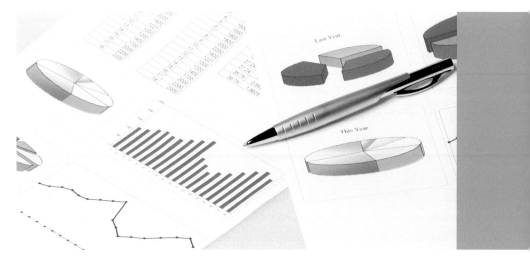

- sales reports
- customer lists
- other reports.

Sources of secondary research:
- census publications
- government department reports
- local authorities
- online databases
- books, newspapers, magazines, journals, etc.

Sources of primary research:
- questionnaires
- interviews
- focus groups
- observations
- experiments.

When listing the methods employed, use impersonal language.
- A questionnaire was devised and distributed to fifty people.
- An interview was carried out with Mr James Burton, Financial Consultant of JKL Ltd.
- A focus group was used.

Make sure that all the methods used are listed, along with all of the sources of secondary research.

Findings

This is the main section of the report. It is here that all the data gathered should be listed. The findings should be concrete facts. Each of the facts listed should have evidence to support it from either the secondary or primary research carried out.

As already mentioned, the findings should be listed as facts. The findings should be written objectively and should be free from bias. When presenting findings be aware of the audience that the report is for. Are there any technical terms that could cause confusion? Don't assume that the reader will understand technical terms. If necessary include a glossary of terms at the end of the report.

If the report has been requested by a specific group or organisation the researcher's job is to show the importance and validity of the research. The report should inform and persuade the audience.

The use of images, diagrams, graphs and tables to present findings can enhance the report, but only use these where relevant.

Clarity of thought and writing is of utmost importance.
- Keep sentences short, clear and simple.
- Avoid using vague or ambiguous expressions.
- Divide findings into sections.
- Use bulleted lists.
- Move on to a new section or paragraph to indicate a new topic.
- Avoid using multiple tenses.

The findings should be organised into sections using multi-level bullet points or outline numbering to indicate sub-sections. Sections should be planned in advance to reveal and expand the central and vital points of the report findings. There should be a logical flow to the sections.

Reflect back on the most important points. Use summaries at the end of sections before moving on to a new theme (Newbury and Swift, 1996).

Analysing questionnaires

As part of the report, questionnaires may have been administered by means of an interview, or through other methods discussed in Section 1. Here you will find instructions on how to analyse questionnaires and present the findings.

Validation

Before the questionnaires can be analysed, they must first be validated. Sometimes questionnaires contain a space for the name and address of the respondent. The reason for this is so that researchers can verify that the person was actually interviewed. The easiest way to validate the questionnaires in a real-world environment is to contact a percentage of the people interviewed. In the case of anonymous questionnaires, this step is ignored.

The next step is to establish whether the respondent should have been interviewed in the first place. Every respondent must meet the interview criteria. This is why there should be a screening question at the beginning of the questionnaire.

Finally, some interviewers may be tempted to ask some questions and just fill in the blanks themselves. In the case of the short structured report, the researcher may also be the interviewer, and he or she will have to ensure that all interviews are valid.

Coding

Now the answers to each question must be coded. The easiest way to analyse a questionnaire is to have all the answers to closed-ended questions pre-coded. Each answer given by each respondent is then gone through and the code related to the answer is attributed.

If the questionnaire contains open-ended questions you can code the answers after the interviews have been administered. To do this:

- List all the responses that were given to the question.
- Group responses that have the same meaning together.
- Assign a code to each response.

Once the coding process has been completed, highlight the appropriate code relating to the answer given by the respondent.

Data entry and analysis

The next step is entering the data into the appropriate computer software, if the college provides this facility. Remember, data on its own is of little use – it has to be converted into meaningful information. Researchers nowadays usually use software for data analysis. It is at this point that a final error check is done. However, for the purposes of the report such data analysis is not necessary, so we can skip to the next step.

Presenting the findings of questionnaires/interviews

Now that the data has been gathered and analysed, the findings can be presented. One method of doing this is to have a frequency table that shows the number of respondents next to each answer that was given. From this table it is possible to present the findings using percentages.

Constructing a frequency table

Question 4 on the sample questionnaire was as follows:

How would you prefer to arrange your trip?   Code
☐   a.   Independently   1
☐   b.   Through your job/studies   2
☐   c.   Tour operator   3
☐   d.   Internet   4

Note the coding on the right-hand side. If a respondent's answer was the internet, the number four would be circled. Colours can be used for the coding process instead of numbers.

Assuming twenty people were interviewed (samples are normally larger than this), the following frequency table demonstrates how the respondents replied:

Independently	1
Through your job/studies	1
Tour operator	8
Internet	10

These findings could also be presented in percentage form as follows:
- 5 per cent stated that they would arrange the trip independently
- 5 per cent would prefer to arrange the trip through job or studies
- 40 per cent would arrange travel using a package tour
- 50 per cent of respondents would organise the trip using the internet.

Cross-tabulation

Cross-tabulation involves looking at the patterns that emerge when answers are analysed. Patterns can emerge among items like gender, age and occupation (McClelland, 1995). With this information to hand, a company could use cross-tabulation to identify its target market for a product or service.

Using charts to present research findings

Findings can be illustrated using charts. The following charts use the results of the frequency table generated from question 4 of the sample survey.

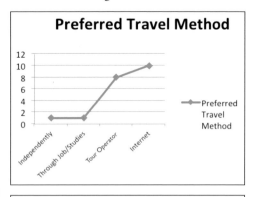

Line Chart/Trend Graph

A trend graph is usually used to show trends in figures, such as sales or unemployment levels over a period of time. Therefore, as the diagram demonstrates, it is not suitable for presenting the results of this question.

Pie Chart

This is a very suitable graph for this type of question. At a glance it is clear to the reader that the internet was the most popular method. Applications like Excel or Word provide options such as displaying values or percentages on the chart.

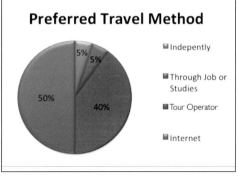

Bar Chart

This is also an effective graph for this question. This type of graph is also used to show trends, such as sales figures for different items from year to year.

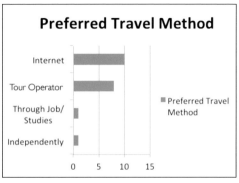

Conclusions

Now that the findings have been presented, conclusions need to be arrived at. The findings should be summarised into three or more points. The conclusions reached in the report must be backed up by the findings. The conclusions should set out answers to the questions in the terms of reference.

In the conclusion, the author of the report is attempting to pull all the findings together into three or four points. Don't simply list all the findings again: gather them into a point supported by the relevant facts. Never introduce a new topic in the conclusion. Ensure a logical pattern is followed where findings have progressed to conclusions. See the sample report in this section as an example of how to form conclusions.

Recommendations

Depending on the type of report undertaken, the author may or may not be required to make recommendations. Three or more recommendations for this report would be sufficient. There should be a logical sequence between findings, conclusions and recommendations.

Recommendations should consist of the author's informed opinion and should be listed in descending order of importance. This means that the most important recommendations should be listed first. To distinguish between conclusions and recommendations, it is worth noting that recommendations are usually in the future tense, as they are a list of proposals for implementation.

Don't group too many recommendations together. List each one separately but keep in mind that too many recommendations can be overpowering. If multiple problems exist, pick out the most important recommendations that should be implemented. Large reports could have several pages of recommendations, but in the short structured report you should limit the number.

The language you use should be clear and positive. If the recommendation is not understood, it can't be implemented. The proposed implementation should be feasible. A company or organisation may not be able to implement a recommendation that is too elaborate or expensive.

The recommendations must address the organisation's needs. If there is a clear link between the terms of reference, findings, conclusions and recommendations, this will be evident to the manager or organisation (Mort, 1992).

Guidelines for producing the report

- Use a serif font, such as Garamond or Times New Roman, as serif fonts are easier to read. Sans-serif fonts such as the Arial family or Verdana are mainly used for display or headings. Avoid script fonts such as Edwardian Script; although they look nice, they are very difficult to read.
- Use size 12pt, or no lower than size 10pt for the body text. Main headings can be 14pt.
- Avoid using too many different fonts and font sizes. Be consistent.
- Enhancements such as **bold** and *italics* can draw attention to text. However, overuse of these can make a document look cluttered and untidy.
- One clear line should be left after every heading if single-line spacing is being used. Leave one clear line between paragraphs.
- Leave one space after a comma and two spaces after a full stop. (The double space after a full stop is a FÁS, FETAC and HETAC requirement: modern publishers do not use it.)
- Use visuals only where relevant.
- Left align or justify the text.
- Keep lines as short as possible.
- Use headings, sub-headings and bullet points (Kolin, 2008).

Appendices

If appendices are included they appear at the back of the report, preceding the bibliography. Appendices consist of material that may need to be referred to by the reader. Examples include extracts from works consulted in the method of procedure, the actual questionnaires that were filled out, or a set of frequency tables showing all the questions with the number of respondents next to each answer.

Bibliography

This is the last part of the report. In this section all books, journals, websites and any other materials consulted should be listed. Software such as EndNote has made creating bibliographies very easy. The citation can be inserted after the text and then the full reference appears in the bibliography automatically. There are also databases of citations on the internet; one such website is http://www.worldcat.org/. This website has a collection of citations for books, journals, etc. and once an account has been created, the user can search for the full citation and export it. You will be given guidelines on what style of referencing to use, for example Harvard style.

The very short report that follows demonstrates how the report writer constructed the conclusions and recommendations from the findings. An analysis follows.

1. **Title:**

   Donnelly Institute of Higher Education

   Report on food poisoning in the staff canteen

2. **Terms of Reference:**

   As requested by management, to investigate the causes of food poisoning in the canteen and to make any necessary recommendations to ensure future safety.

3. **Method of Procedure:**

   The catering manager was interviewed.

   A questionnaire was devised and distributed in the staff canteen.

   The equipment was analysed.

4. **Findings:**

   - The catering manager was on holidays during the period in question and nobody was left in charge. As a result nobody took responsibility for the cleanliness of the canteen.
   - The equipment was found to be up to date with industry standards and in working order.
   - The equipment was not cleaned regularly enough.
   - Staff are not fully aware of the procedures for cleaning the equipment.
   - Utensils were not being cleaned properly.
   - Raw meat and cooked meat were left on the same surfaces as staff are not aware of food safety practices.

5. **Conclusions:**

   - The management procedures were inadequate.
   - Staff are not aware of cleaning procedures.
   - Basic food safety procedures are not being followed.

6. **Recommendations:**
   - A rota should be in place for supervising the kitchen.
   - Staff should be informed about cleaning and food safety procedures.
   - Implement a chart system that staff have to sign at different times of the day to ensure that procedures are being followed.
   - Management structures need to be in place to ensure the kitchen is supervised while the catering manager is absent.

Report presented by Jake Williams
10 January 2011

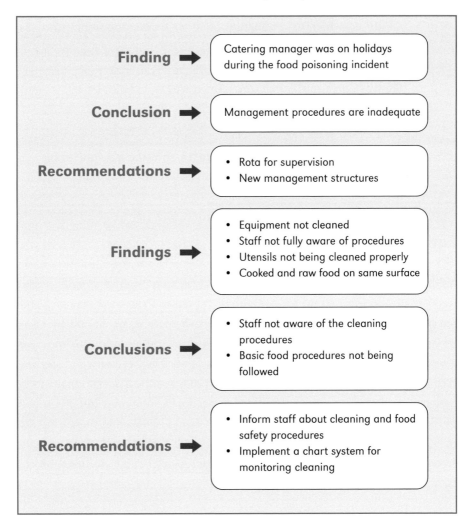

Report analysis

- The report is written using impersonal language and without bias.
- The conclusions and recommendations are the writer's informed opinion. This is demonstrated in the diagrams above.

Exercises

1. List the elements that should be contained in a short structured report.

2. What are the most important rules for presenting findings?

3. A report was presented to management and after reading it management felt that the conclusions did not make any sense. Can you think of any reason why this might be so?

4. Explain how the findings of questionnaires and interviews are analysed and list briefly the ways in which they can be presented.

5. Using the flow diagram as a template, show how a conclusion and recommendation can be formulated from findings.

Summary

The report is worth one-quarter of the overall marks for the communications module and will probably be the assignment that takes up the most time. Therefore, students are advised, first, to take on a topic related to their vocational area and, second, to choose a topic of personal interest to them. Care should be taken when deciding on the method of research. Don't be too ambitious. If the main aim of the report is to provide information, it may be necessary to carry out secondary research only. Other types of report may require a questionnaire to be designed. Follow the guidelines outlined in Section 1. The most important part of the report is the findings section, and care should be taken in presenting this in a visually pleasing way. Finally, make sure that the conclusions and the recommendations of the report are formulated logically and are based on the facts gathered.

SECTION 3

Business Documents

Introduction

No matter what career a person ends up choosing, chances are they will come across business documents on a weekly or even daily basis. You may also be required to produce a business document such as a letter or a memo, or may have to sit in on a meeting and take the minutes. Therefore, as part of the written communication section, this book will go through these documents. The following business documents will be covered.

- Memorandum, more commonly known as a 'memo'.
- Documents for meetings:
    - notice

- agenda
- minutes.
- Business letter.

Memorandum

The memo is a form of written communication widely used in organisations. A memo is usually only a few lines long and is commonly used to communicate general messages to staff.

With the use of word processing applications such as Microsoft Word, memos are easy to generate by means of a template. Whatever the template, the information required for a memo is the same. The first part of the memo should state who it is for, the sender, the date and the subject. There should be also a 'c.c.' field (carbon copy), if copies of the memo have been sent to anybody else.

The second part of the memo is the message being communicated.

EXAMPLE

MEMORANDUM

To: All users of the canteen
From: J. Mahon, Manager
Date: 2 April 2011
Subject: Use of utensils, cutlery and equipment

It has been brought to my attention by users of the canteen that basic rules are not being adhered to. I would like to remind all users that every person must supply their own delph, cutlery, etc. Also, as the centre's canteen is being used by many different organisations, some companies have asked me to remind you that each company must supply their own kitchen equipment such as toasters, microwaves, kettles, etc.

I thank you in advance for your co-operation.

Documents for meetings

Three documents in this section are related to the meeting. (The verbal and non-verbal communication in relation to meetings has been dealt with in other sections of this book.) The secretary of the company or organisation is responsible for the preparation and distribution of these documents. The notice and agenda are prepared by the secretary in advance of the meeting. Notes are taken by the secretary during the meeting, and the minutes are prepared from these notes. We will now look at each document separately.

The notice

A notice is a short, simple message stating when a meeting will take place, along with the time and the venue. It should be sent out prior to the meeting, giving the participants plenty of time to make arrangements so that they will be able to attend. The secretary is usually responsible for sending out the notice of the meeting and ensuring that every member receives it.

The notice can be in the form of a memo, letter or email. Rather than sending out a notice to each member, it can be displayed on the organisation's message board. It should be proofread for accuracy and to make sure that the essential information has been provided. If possible, a reminder should be sent out a day or two before the meeting, either by phone or by email.

EXAMPLE

Dear Member

There will be a staff meeting on Friday, 12 March 2011 at 10.30 a.m. in the staff canteen. The agenda for this meeting is attached. All staff are expected to attend.

Julia Smith
Secretary

- Type the salutation – Dear Member.
- Leave one clear line.
- Type the details (event, date, time, venue, etc.).
- Leave four lines clear for signing.
- Type the word 'Secretary'.

The agenda

This document is usually sent out with the notice of the meeting. It contains, in order, all the items for discussion. This is an important document and is necessary for the smooth and orderly running of a meeting. Sending out the agenda with the notice gives participants the opportunity to prepare for the meeting in advance. The first four items contained in the agenda for a meeting are standard and are listed below.

1. Apologies for Absence
   - Here the chairperson will list the people who are unable to attend and have sent their apologies.
2. Minutes of the Last Meeting
   - The chairperson reads out the minutes of the last meeting. The minutes must then be approved and signed.
3. Matters Arising from the Minutes
   - Here the chairperson will give participants the opportunity to comment on or provide any information on outstanding matters arising from the last meeting.
4. Correspondence
   - The chairperson will ask the secretary to read out or summarise any correspondence the organisation has received since the last meeting.

After these four items, new items up for discussion are listed. Finally, the last two items on the agenda are:

5. Any Other Business (AOB)
   - This gives participants the opportunity to raise matters that were not on the meeting's agenda. If a serious topic is raised and the committee runs out of time, it should be put on the agenda for the next meeting.

6. Date of the Next Meeting
    - This gives members the opportunity to agree a suitable date and time for the next meeting. However, if this proves too difficult, the matter should be decided by the secretary.

EXAMPLE

J Mahon Computers Ltd
Burke Industrial Estate, Cobh
Tel 021 00000
www.mahoncomputers.com
info@jmahon.com

AGENDA

1   Apologies for Absence
2   Minutes of the Previous Meeting
3   Matters Arising from the Minutes
4   Correspondence
5   Department Sales Targets
6   Advertising Campaign for New Product Launch
7   Any Other Business
8   Date of Next Meeting

It is important that the agenda of a meeting is well thought out. If there is a small amount of time allocated for a meeting, such as a staff meeting, then any pressing issues should get priority. An agenda should not have too many items up for discussion as participants may get irritable when a meeting goes over the time allotted. This may result in participants not giving important issues their full attention.

Recommendations for formatting an agenda
- The company or organisation should form the header of the page. Use the same information that would be contained in a letterhead, i.e. the address, phone number, website and email address.
- Leave at least two clear lines after the company or organisation information.

- Type the heading 'Agenda'.
- List the topics in order of discussion.

Minutes of the meeting

The secretary is responsible for taking notes during the meeting. Notes should be taken under each agenda heading. Only the main points need to be recorded. In the section of this book dealing with message taking, you learned to distinguish between essential and non-essential information. The same applies here. The secretary needs to be able to distinguish between relevant and irrelevant information. When shorthand was more widely used, secretaries took down the notes in shorthand and then wrote them out again in longhand. Nowadays the minutes of the meeting are typed up from the notes. It is recommended that the secretary types up the minutes as soon as possible while the information is fresh. Another advantage of this procedure is that the minutes can be posted or emailed to any member who requests them. Therefore, the minutes can be easily provided to any member who was unable to attend.

EXAMPLE

The following is an example of how the minutes are written. The headings are taken from the sample agenda.

Minutes of the Management Meeting
held on Friday 12 March 2011
at 10.30 a.m.
in the company offices

Present
J. Mahon (Chairperson)
K. Lyons (Secretary)
T. Turner
M. Stevenson

J. Barry

A. Nolan

1. Apologies for Absence
    Apologies from K. Maher and M. Foley.

2. Minutes of the Previous Meeting
    The minutes of the meeting held on Friday, 12 February at 10.30
    a.m. were read, approved and signed.

3. Matters Arising from the Minutes
    In the last meeting it was decided that floppy disks should be
    removed from the shelves as it was felt that most customers use
    memory keys or CDs for storage purposes. However, T. Turner
    brought it to the chairperson's attention that a number of teachers
    have requested floppy disks for use in exams and as a consequence
    of this it is recommended that a small stock of floppy disks be
    kept for the foreseeable future for this market.

4. Correspondence
    Correspondence from Dell, Compaq and HP was read by the
    secretary. The companies are launching computers with new
    operating systems.

5. Department Sales Targets
    The following targets were set for the month of April for each
    department:
    Game Consoles – €30,000
    PCs and Laptops – €60,000
    Software Department – €16,000
    Computer Accessories Department – €20,000

6. Advertising Campaign for New Product Launch
M. Stevenson and J. Barry suggested that the company should advertise the new product on the local radio station. A. Nolan suggested that a flyer should be sent to the local newspapers advertising the new product along with other special offers in the store. The rest of the management team agreed.

7. Any Other Business
M. Stevenson suggested that the staff party due to be held on 24 April be postponed until summer and the party be used as a team-building event. All the other members agreed. T. Turner raised the issue of social networking and whether or not the company should start advertising on Facebook and Twitter. It was decided that this matter be put on the agenda for the next meeting.

8. Date of the Next Meeting
The next meeting will be held on Friday 16 April at 10.30 a.m. in the company's office.

Recommendations for formatting the minutes
- The first line of the minutes should state the time, date and place that the meeting was held.
- Leave one clear line. Type a list of members who were present at the meeting.
- Leave one clear line. Type the heading 'Apologies' and list the names of those who could not attend.
- Use the agenda headings to type up the rest of the minutes. Type the heading and directly underneath list what was discussed in relation to the topic.

Tip: When typing up the minutes in Microsoft Word, use a numbered list. Word automatically goes to the next number when the enter key is pressed, but to prevent this from happening, enter a 'soft return' by holding down the shift key and pressing the enter key simultaneously. Then you can continue typing what was discussed under the relevant heading.

The business letter

A business letter should be written in a formal manner. The letter should be succinct. The author needs to be specific and the letter should be accurate. In many cases the business letter you write might be the first written communication a company or individual receives from your company or organisation. Therefore, it is important to make a good impression.

There are many different types of business letter; they include:
- letter of inquiry
- sales letter
- letter of complaint
- letter of acknowledgement (acknowledging a letter already received)
- letter to debtors requesting payment.

There are various styles of business letter but the most up-to-date is fully blocked with open punctuation. This means that paragraphs are not indented and there is no punctuation at the end of the address lines and following salutation and closing. Some companies also use headed paper with the company details as a letterhead at the top of the page. The following section shows an example of this type of letter.

Aspen Motors
Tralee, Co. Kerry • Tel 066-7120000
Email:aspen@eircom.net   www.aspen.com

Our ref: JM/AM

Your ref: MT/JK

20 June 2011

Mr John O'Connell
10 High St
Tralee
Co. Kerry

Dear Mr O'Connell

Thank you for your enquiry about the Opel Corsa car range. We have pleasure in enclosing a brochure and price list detailing all information about the six cars in the range.

We would be delighted if you would call to our branch to discuss your requirements and we will gladly arrange test drives. A scrappage deal is in place and, should you require, finance options are available. If you feel that the new models don't meet your budget, we also have an excellent selection of second-hand vehicles.

We look forward to meeting you in the near future.

Yours sincerely

James McCarthy

James McCarthy
Sales Department

Enc.

Notes on the sample business letter

- The first section is the letterhead.
- This is followed by references; the first reference is the sender's, two clear lines are left, and the second is the recipient's. Leave two clear lines after the references.
- The date is now entered, and it should be written in full. Again two clear lines are left.
- Enter the recipient's name and address. Two clear lines are left again.
- This is followed by the salutation; usually the name is in the form of title followed by surname.
- The body of the letter is divided into paragraphs, with one clear line dividing them.
- The first paragraph outlines the reason for the letter, the second provides any additional details and the last paragraph contains an expected outcome.
- The author then signs off the letter. 'Yours sincerely' is used when the recipient's name is known, whereas 'Yours faithfully' is used if it isn't.
- Leave enough room for a signature, usually four clear lines.
- If there is an enclosure, indicate this by putting 'Enc.' at the end of the letter, with two clear lines before it.
- Spacing rules tend to vary but be consistent with whatever rules you choose.

Summary

Companies differ in the format of their business documents. It is important that you familiarise yourself with the correct layout of the business documents associated with your organisation, and be consistent in any written communication to other organisations, companies or individuals.

Exercises

1. Write a memo to your class, detailing that there will be a student council meeting next Thursday at 11.00 a.m. in room 302.

2. Write up a notice and agenda for the above meeting.

3. As a group, run a mock meeting for the above agenda. Take notes from the meeting and each individual student should write up the minutes of the meeting.

SECTION 4

Personal Writing

Learning Outcomes

Learners will:
- be able to write a personal letter
- be able to write a short story.

Introduction

The use of personal letters has certainly decreased, but people still like receiving them and they still have their place in written communication. A piece of personal writing must be included as part of the collection of work for the communications module. This section will go through different types of personal letters and give guidelines for creative writing, i.e. writing a short story.

Letters

The personal letters covered in this section are:
- letter of thanks
- letter of condolence
- letter of congratulations
- letter of complaint.

Letter of thanks

A letter of thanks is written to convey gratitude. A letter of thanks might be thanking somebody for a present or some kind action. It might also be a letter acknowledging an invitation to a function.

Format of letter of thanks

- The first paragraph gives the reason for the letter, so thank the person in the first section of the letter.
  - Thank you so much for driving me to the airport last week; I really appreciated it.
  - Thank you very much for your beautiful gift.
- The next paragraph can give some extra information, for example news about yourself since the last time you were talking to the person or something related to the last time you communicated with the person.
- Sign off the letter with a complimentary close such as 'all the best'.

Letter of condolence

A letter of condolence is not an easy letter to write as it can cause sadness to the sender and the recipient. There are different types of letters of condolence, for example to somebody who has been in a serious accident, or to somebody who has lost their job. However, this text will focus on a letter of condolence to a person who has lost a loved one. A letter of condolence is suitable if you are unable to attend the funeral service or express your condolences in person.

Format of letter of condolence

- Start the letter by expressing how sad you were to hear of their loss; for example:
  - I was deeply saddened to hear of the death of ...

- We were very sorry to hear about the death of ...
- It is inappropriate to include any recent news about yourself in this case. In the next paragraph it is acceptable to include some memories of the person, and words of comfort, for example:
  - We were all very fond of him. He was so full of life and such a good friend.
- If you feel you can be of any assistance to the person, include this in the last paragraph.

Letter of congratulations

This letter congratulates somebody – for example a person who has recently passed their exams, got engaged, got married, had a new baby, moved to a new home or started a new job – the list is endless.

Format of letter of congratulations

- This letter is very similar to the letter of thanks, the only difference being the first paragraph, which will be to congratulate the person. For example:
  - Congratulations on passing your exams; we knew you could do it!
  - We were so delighted to hear the good news of the birth of your baby girl.
- The other paragraphs are similar to the letter of thanks.

Letter of complaint

A letter of complaint can be written to an organisation, retailer or service provider. When writing a letter of complaint it is important to stick to the facts, and be very clear and to the point.

Format of letter of complaint

● If complaining about a product or service, start off by detailing when you bought the product or service, and specify that you are including a copy of the receipt if you still have it.

● Next specify exactly what the problem is with the product or service.

● Finish by expressing the expected outcome of the letter. For example, state that you would like a full cash refund.

EXAMPLE

The following is an example of a personal letter.

14 Current Street
Mallow
Co Cork

10 November 2011

Dear Mary

Thank you so much for the beautiful iPod Touch with fifty songs that you sent me. It's fantastic! You definitely have my taste in music spot on!

I hope you enjoyed the party. Sorry I didn't get to chat with you properly. I had no idea that Mom and Dad had invited so many people! I have been really busy with college. The first semester exams are after Christmas so unfortunately I will have to study over the holidays.

I am really looking forward to seeing you over the holidays. Tell all the folks I said hello.

All the best
Breda

Summary

Handwritten personal letters may become a thing of the past, but the same formats can be adopted for emails, sending messages through social networking websites, etc.

Short story

You can improve your writing skills even more – and enjoy yourself at the same time – by writing creatively. Writing short stories can be both easy and difficult: easy because of the length of time it takes to write them compared to a novel; difficult because the author has to develop a theme, plot, character(s) and point of view in a few short pages. The following are some guidelines to help write a short story.

- A short story generally has the following elements: introduction, conflict, rising action, climax and conclusion. The beginning and end of the story should be the strongest parts.
- Begin the story by establishing a specific time and place. The opening paragraph should set the scene of a particular event.
- The central character should be involved in the story from the beginning. The story should be told from the central character's point of view. The point of view can be written in the first or third person. First person point of view is more personal.
- There should be a theme to the story, an underlying message. There should be few characters; too many characters can take away from the main theme of the story.
- The time frame should be short. It should cover one main event in the life of a character. It is very difficult to cover years of a character's life in a short story.
- The story should have a combination of characters, thoughts and actions as well as some dialogue. Thoughts and actions are more effective than too much dialogue.
- Every phrase or sentence in a short story should have a purpose. The purpose should be to build character or develop the plot.
- Conflict should be introduced early in the story. The focus then is on how the character will be able to resolve the conflict. The climax of the story should be near the end.

- The plot should be developed through characters. The narrator should not interfere.
- To keep the reader's interest, each paragraph should begin with the character(s) in action. When describing the action the character is involved in, the narrator should avoid including too much background information as this can frustrate the reader. The information should instead be included in the action.
- The ending of a story should not be forced. If it is not clear to the narrator what path the main character should take, the story should be put aside until it becomes apparent.
- Finally, revise the first draft of the story. Every word should have a purpose, be accurate and provide character detail. This will tighten up the story. (Wiehardt, n.d.)

The following is a short story written by a Leaving Certificate student named Eoghan O'Sullivan. Read the story. How did the author use the guidelines provided above?

Train Journey

by
Eoghan O'Sullivan

Hiss-hiss-shudder. The steady vibration of the train's wheels against the steel track passed through the floor and sides of the carriage, jolting the side of Michael's head gently against the window. He was sitting turned towards the aisle of the carriage, his right elbow resting on the table in front of him.

Outside, the landscape of Dublin's suburbs streamed by, grey with only an occasional flash of green breaking the steady monotony. The sky was its perpetual leaden hue, pushing down on the city below, lending the entire scene a sullen cast. But the view held little interest for Michael: he had other things on his mind.

The white wires of an iPod trailed from his ears, the tinny sound of Guns n' Roses audible from the far side of the carriage. It was raw, visceral music, full of the energy and anger of youth. Right at this moment it matched his mood perfectly.

Michael had had another row with his mother, the third in two weeks. Anger burned in his chest as he sat there, running it through his mind again and again and again. These days they couldn't seem to sit in the same room without arguing about something, anything even. It wasn't that he enjoyed fighting with her, or even that he set out to do so; it just seemed to happen.

He'd seen this one coming though, that he would freely admit. He walked home from school far slower than normal that afternoon, lingering on the way, hoping to delay the inevitable. He knew what was going to happen and would have done anything to avoid it. But, as always happened at moments like this, no immediately obvious alternative presented itself, so he had little choice but to continue.

The recently painted surface of the front door felt tacky under his fingers as he pushed it open and entered, walking through the narrow carpeted hallway and on into the kitchen, hoping to grab some food and quickly vanish to his room, safely out of range for the time being. Within seconds of entering the kitchen, however, his hopes were dashed. Michael sighed inwardly; the letter from school lay on the kitchen table, his report sitting unfolded beside it. There was going to be trouble, he could feel it.

'Mick?' his mother said, sounding weary as she spoke, 'Please sit down.'

He turned to face her, he'd had no idea she was there. She was sitting up against the far wall of the kitchen, out of sight from the front door. With dismay he registered his father sitting there as well, managing to look both stern and embarrassed at the same time. Oh Jesus. His dad had gotten off work early for this? It couldn't be that bad – could it?

He didn't sit. The atmosphere in the room was far too oppressive for that.

'What?' he replied, pretending, in defiance of all probability, that he hadn't noticed what was clearly sitting on the table. 'What's wrong now?'

'You know full well what's wrong, don't try acting stupid. Or would you like to try taking a wild guess?'

'My report came.'

'Oh, well done. Got it first try. Would you like to take another guess as to what you actually got?'

'Dunno.'

'You got one C, three Ds and failed three subjects. Do you think that's good enough? Because I certainly don't.'

She'd started ranting at that point. Going on and on without expecting him to respond, and without really caring whether he did or not. Michael couldn't really remember what she'd said; it didn't matter to him much anyway. He'd heard it all before, more times than he would have cared to.

His father had sat there the whole time, not saying a word, just looking at the two of them and growing visibly more uncomfortable as the minutes passed. Michael found himself becoming angrier with him than he was with his mother. Did he have to just sit there, nothing but so much dead weight? If he wasn't going to say anything why was he here? To give this lecture some appearance of parental unity? Well, he'd failed if that was the idea. He'd had nothing to do with it, that much was obvious.

Michael stood up, growing angrier as his mother continued. Eventually he turned, and without saying a word left the kitchen, heading for the front door.

His father got to his feet, uttering his first words since Michael had arrived.

'Don't you leave,' he said, trying to summon some authority. 'Don't you dare!'

Michael carried on out of the house, not caring what he or anyone else had to say. He slammed the door behind him and started walking, going in the direction of the train station.

Now, on the train, sitting on the awful blue-and-yellow patterned seats, a plan began to form in his mind. He was going to go into Dublin and stay there until late that evening, not answering his phone. Let them worry about him, he didn't care. Maybe that would change their reaction to his report. A nasty smile split his face as he thought of it. He might not even go home that night at all; he could sleep in one of his friend's houses. Yeah, that was an idea. That would definitely wake them up a bit, make them suffer.

As he considered his plan, the song playing on his iPod ended and the next began. Pavarotti. He paused, shaken from thoughts of his triumph by the opera music. He wished his dad wouldn't put his music on the computer; most of it was dire, and sometimes it ended up on Michael's iPod. He reached into his pocket to change songs.

The iPod slipped from his grasp as he pulled it from his uniform trousers

and bounced off his leg before landing on the carpeted floor of the carriage, pulling the headphones from his ears. He cursed and reached down to recover it.

He stopped, his arm outstretched, fingers brushing the smooth surface of the iPod. There was something else. Michael looked closer. It was a small black rucksack, tucked under his seat. He sat up again for a moment and looked around the carriage, trying to work out who it might belong to. But no one really stood out. He was alone except for an old couple, a woman with grey hair and a man whose hair was slowly deserting him, his hairline receding up towards his scalp. They were sitting on the opposite side of the carriage, four rows down, reading the paper to one another. Someone must have left the bag behind, forgotten it as they left the train.

Michael grasped the bag, hoisting it onto the table with a thud. If he'd been asked at that moment exactly what he was planning, he wouldn't have known. There was no coherent thought behind his actions, they were driven by simple curiosity. The tough material of the bag rustled as he closed his hand around the zip and pulled it open.

He pushed his hand into the bag and took out the item nearest the top, a plastic lunchbox containing a chocolate bar wrapper and a half eaten apple. He placed it on the tabletop before reaching in again. This time he withdrew a crumpled paperback novel: *Carrie* by Stephen King. A book he'd tried reading before but hadn't stuck with long; altogether too weird for his taste. With increasing impatience he opened the top of the bag to let in more light. He peered in; it had to have *something* interesting in it. It did. Lying on the bottom of the bag he could make out two roughly oblong shapes. He looked closer, and a wall of surprise and disbelief crashed over him, smacking into his head and chest like a blow from a baseball bat.

Shock flooded through his body, coursing on his skin with a tingling sensation. At the bottom of the bag were twin bundles of one hundred euro notes, each bound with an elastic band. It occurred to him he was holding more money than he'd ever had in his life. Terrified someone would see what it contained, he shoved the bag down between his legs, his head snapping up, eyes darting around the carriage, his breathing fast.

Slowly he began to calm. It was still just him and the aging couple, and their attentions were still fixed on their newspapers. As his heart rate began to slow, he was struck by the decision now facing him. He couldn't take the bag, or even all of the money. No one carried around that much cash for honest reasons, least of all in a rucksack, and the last thing he wanted was for drug-dealers to find out that he'd stolen their money. But he couldn't let an opportunity like this pass him by – he *never* had money.

The opposing forces of greed and fear duelled within him, neither gaining the upper hand. A compromise would have to do. He counted out both piles, not taking them out of the bag. There were thirty bank notes in one, the other held thirty-two. Michael took two of the pale green notes from each pile, folded them carefully and placed them in his pocket. A furtive grin stole across his face as he did so, once again glancing around the carriage. With luck the owner wouldn't notice the missing cash, assuming they recovered their bag. And if they did, the thought of theft mightn't occur to them.

Michael replaced the bag under his seat, stood, and left the carriage, walking past the couple on his way out. He'd sit somewhere else. Just in case the owner came back and found him sitting over the bag with four hundred euro in his pockets. That would take a little explaining, to say the least. A wild glee came over him as he sat down again, two carriages down. He was *rich* – well, relatively at least. He couldn't believe what had just happened, a whole raft of new possibilities stretching out before him. In the light of his sudden discovery, storming out of the house was beginning to look like the best decision he had ever made. A quiet laugh bubbled from Michael's mouth, still coming to terms with his good luck.

There was a purpose to his movement as he left the train, pushing through the milling crowds on the platform before making his way onto the street. Michael felt a pressing need to spend some of his new-found wealth; to treat himself. Excitement filled him, and within minutes he was standing outside a clothes shop, its façade a mass of glass and concrete. A security guard stood outside, wearing a thick coat against the cold of the evening. Michael had decided that the first thing he needed was decent clothes; the school uniform had to be shed.

The automatic doors hissed apart as Michael approached, warm heated air from the shop's interior tickling at his face as it escaped past him. The shop was largely empty; only the occasional customer could be seen, drifting through the brightly lit landscape of racks and aisles. A quick scan of the shop directed him to the menswear.

Within fifteen minutes he had what he wanted: a hoody, t-shirt and jeans. He'd little choice but to stick with his school shoes for the time being; carrying his uniform around was going to present him with enough of a problem. And he didn't want to spend too much of the money just yet; having it in his pocket gave him an intoxicating feeling of power, one which he wanted to experience for just a little longer.

There was no one else queuing so he walked directly up to the sales desk, a bored-looking cashier standing behind it. Michael placed the clothes on the desk and began reaching into his pocket for the money.

'Just these.'

She scanned the clothes, using a magnet built into the faux wood of the desk to remove the security tags. 'That'll be a hundred and thirty-eight euro fifty. Would you like a bag?'

'Eh, yeah. I could probably use one.' Michael slid two of the hundred euro notes across the counter. 'Thanks.'

Her eyes narrowed slightly at the sight of the notes, her face losing its bored look. She picked them up, and then moved them behind the counter, holding them out of sight for a few moments. She looked up again and smiled, meeting his eye for the first time in their entire exchange.

'I'm sorry, but I don't have the right change for this. Would it be okay if I went and got my supervisor to refill my till?'

'Yeah, sure, whatever.'

She vanished into the back of the shop. Michael was left standing at the counter, and within a minute had grown impatient. What could be taking her so *long*? He shifted his upper body slightly, neck craning in a vain attempt to glimpse into the rear of the shop. He sighed, his fingers drumming on the counter, his eyes reading the various staff announcements taped to the wall without registering their actual meaning.

A large hand descended onto his shoulder, gripping tightly. Michael jumped from the shock, his heart suddenly pounding in his chest. He turned his head, in his fear expecting to see the rightful owner of the money he'd just spent. He had no idea what they looked like of course, but this problem presented his imagination with little difficulty. It was more than capable of providing a whole host of potential villains all on its own: someone huge, probably with tattoos. Michael's stomach clenched at the thought, fear filling his mouth with a coppery taste.

His apprehender came into view. He looked into the grim, unsmiling face of the security guard he'd seen earlier.

'All right, lad, come with me,' the man said, lifting a section of the counter and leading him into the back of the shop.

'What? What's wrong?' Michael replied, his feet propelling him in the direction he was pushed, too numb to resist. 'I haven't stolen anything.'

'Just come with me.' The words brooked no argument.

Michael was brought to a small, sparsely furnished room which contained only a chair and a desk. The security guard told him to sit and then left, returning a few minutes later. He ran a hand through his hair, placed a pair of hundred euro notes on the table, and began to speak.

'Do you recognise these?'

'Yeah, I used them to pay for my clothes,' Michael said, by now utterly confused.

'Well, they're counterfeit. We have a scanner behind the counter. The check-out people see so few of the big notes that they always check them.' He paused and took a breath. 'You do realise that attempting to buy stuff with counterfeit cash is a *crime*? A serious one at that. You're in a whole heap of trouble.'

Michael sat there, his face growing pale as the security guard spoke. He felt a warm pressure building behind his eyes; he was going to start crying if he wasn't careful.

He looked up. 'But I didn't know they were fake,' he insisted, 'it's not my fault.'

The man snorted, something verging on contempt in his eyes.

'Look, don't waste it on me. The Guards have been called. They'll be here in a few minutes. Explain it to them.'

Michael struggled to grasp what had happened. It was just too much to take in. A single tear crept over the rim of his eyelid and began to trickle down his cheek. A feeling of utter helplessness had come over him, making even the slightest movement seem an effort. He opened his mouth and spoke, a pleading tone in his voice.

'Can I please call my parents?'

Summary

Handwritten personal letters may become a thing of the past, but the same formats can be adopted for emails, sending messages through social networking sites, etc. Writing short stories is a great way for individuals to express themselves. Overall, personal writing is a great means of personal development. Short stories, poems, even daily notes in your diary all give you an opportunity to express yourself. Your skill at writing will grow the more you use it.

Exercises

1. Write a letter of thanks to your friend, Mary. She sent you a lovely present for your birthday. Mention some news about yourself in the letter.

2. You bought a new dress in a local clothes shop called 'Fancy Fashions'. After taking the dress home you noticed that a section of the dress had come apart at the seams. Write a suitable letter of complaint stating that you would like a full cash refund.

3. Write a story based on a real public event (such as a match, concert, etc.), involving two characters who meet for the first time that day.

Grammar and Punctuation

Introduction

Grammar and punctuation are very important in written communication. This section will first look at some of the parts of speech, and then look at punctuation.

Parts of speech

The following are the main parts of speech:
- nouns
- pronouns

- adjectives
- verbs
- adverbs.

Noun

A noun is a word that represents a person, place, thing or idea.

Noun	Examples
Names	Joe Murphy, Mary Adams
	girl, woman, man, boy
Place names	Dundalk, New York, Switzerland
Common names in location	park, town, village
Things	computer, car, football
Ideas	freedom, happiness

Pronoun

A pronoun is used to replace a noun. It can refer back to a noun mentioned in a previous sentence. Examples are: I, you, he, she, it, me, you, him, her, us, them, mine, your, his, her and their.

Adjective

An adjective is used to describe a noun. Here are some examples.

The *big* house.
The *blue* car.
He has *black* hair.
She is *tall*.

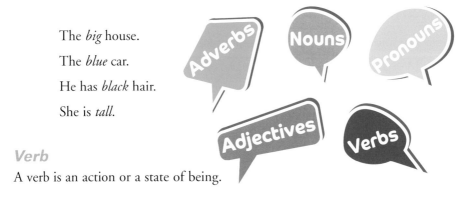

Verb

A verb is an action or a state of being.

State of being – the verb 'to be'

I am

You are

She/He is

We are

Ye/You are

They are

Examples of sentences with verbs:

I *ran* down the road.

He *cut* the lawn.

We *went* to town.

I *am* tired.

Adverbs

An adverb is used to describe a verb or adjective. Examples:

I am very cold – 'cold' is the adjective and 'very' is the adverb.

She is very sick – 'sick' is the adjective and 'very' is the adverb.

I am awfully sorry – 'sorry' is the adjective and 'awfully' is the adverb.

He is extremely quiet – 'quiet' is the adjective and 'extremely' is the adverb.

I ran quickly – 'ran' is the verb and 'quickly' is the adverb.

The song is finally over – 'over' is the adjective and 'finally' is the adverb.

Prepositions

Prepositions are used in a sentence to show location or time or direction and they have a relationship with a noun or pronoun in the sentence. Examples:

The cars are coming *towards* us.

Tim was hiding *under* the table.

After dinner, we watched television.

I fell asleep *on* the couch.

I nearly fell *down* the stairs.

Punctuation

The most common use of punctuation is to indicate where a pause should occur in a sentence. When sentences are said out loud natural pauses occur, whereas in written communication, pauses need to be indicated.

End of sentence punctuation marks

. full stop

! exclamation mark

? question mark

The full stop is used to indicate that the sentence is finished. Variations of the full stop are the exclamation mark and the question mark. The exclamation mark is used when the author of the sentence wants to communicate some feeling, or emphasise something. For example: 'How dare you!' or 'Oh my God!' A question mark is put at the end of a sentence to indicate a question. For example: 'What do you want to do later?'

When typing, no spaces are left before a full stop, exclamation mark or question mark and two spaces are left after (according to FÁS guidelines). Full stops are also used to indicate the initials of a person, company or abbreviation. However, full stops are not necessary for abbreviations/acronyms like Ltd, OECD, ESRI, CSO.

Other punctuation marks

, comma   ; semi-colon

: colon   - hyphen

' apostrophe   '' quotation marks

The comma

The comma is used to indicate a small pause in a sentence. It is also used to separate a list of words in a sentence or to separate two phrases. Examples:

After their day at the seaside, the children were exhausted.
I would like apples, oranges, bananas and grapes from the shop.
He is tall, dark and handsome.

The following are the main uses of a comma.
- To separate words that are part of a series.
- To separate adjectives when more than one adjective is used to describe something.
- In dialogue where a person is addressed directly, for example: 'Sean, will you go to the shop for me?'
- To separate the month from the year:
  The event is on Thursday, 17 July, 2010.
- To separate the lines of an address:
  My address is 10 O'Connell St, Limerick.

The semi-colon

The following are the main uses of a semi-colon.
- To separate parts of a sentence when the individual parts include commas. Example:

  We visited Tralee, Co. Kerry; Clifden, Co. Galway; and Swords, Co. Dublin.

- To join two clauses together if those clauses are related. Example:

  This is one complete sentence; this is another one.

The colon

The following are the main uses of a colon:
- As illustrated here, to introduce a list of bullet points or a numbered list.
- To introduce an example to illustrate an item that is being discussed in the text.
- Preceding a direct quotation.

Quotation marks

Quotation marks are used for direct quotations only. When other punctuation marks such as full stops, commas or question marks are part of the quotation, they should be placed inside the quotation marks. When a quotation is very long, the quotation marks can be omitted and the quote can instead be introduced using a colon and set out from the main text.

The apostrophe

There are two main uses of the apostrophe:

- To show possession, for example:
  John's car.
  Mary's handbag.
  There is one exception, and that is showing a possession belonging to 'It'. For example: The car is a good make. Its colour is blue. Here the 'Its' does not have an apostrophe.
- The apostrophe can also be used to replace letters, for example: I don't, instead of I do not. It's, instead of It is.

The hyphen

A hyphen is used to join a prefix to a word, for example co-operation, or to join two or more words together, for example daughter-in-law. A hyphen is also used in numbers or fractions, for example twenty-three, two-thirds. In general, if you are unsure whether or not the words should have a hyphen between them, leave them as separate words (Straus, 2008).

Spelling

The following is a list of the most commonly misspelled words as identified by Oxford English Dictionaries.

accommodate accommodation	Fahrenheit	occasion	truly
achieve	familiar	occurred occurring	unforeseen
across	finally	occurrence	unfortunately
aggressive aggression	fluorescent	pavilion	until
apparently	foreign	persistent	weird

appearance	foreseeable	pharaoh	wherever
argument	forty	piece	which
assassination	forward	politician	
basically	friend	Portuguese	
beginning	further	possession	
believe	gist	preferred preferring	
bizarre	glamorous	propaganda	
business	government	publicly	
calendar	guard	really	
Caribbean	happened	receive	
cemetery	harass harassment	referred referring	
chauffeur	honorary	religious	
colleague	humorous	remember	
coming	idiosyncrasy	resistance	
committee	immediately	sense	
completely	incidentally	separate	
conscious	independent	siege	
curiosity	interrupt	successful	
definitely	irresistible	supersede	
dilemma	knowledge	surprise	
disappear	liaise, liaison	tattoo	
disappoint	lollipop	tendency	
ecstasy	millennium millennia	therefore	
embarrass	Neanderthal	threshold	
environment	necessary	tomorrow	
existence	noticeable	tongue	

Spell check

Word-processing applications provide spelling and grammar checks. To get the full use of these tools, the computer should be set to the correct region. The steps to access this on the Windows 7 operating system is as follows:

1. Click on the start button and choose the control panel.
2. From the options given, select Clock, Language and Region.
3. Select Region and Language.
4. The Region and Language window should now be visible. Make sure that the format is English (Ireland).
5. Click Apply followed by OK and close the window.

Selecting the spell check from Microsoft Word 2007:

1. Select the review tab in the ribbon.
2. Choose Spelling & Grammar from the proofing group.
3. Make sure the dictionary language is set to English (Ireland) as shown in the dialogue box below.
4. The misspelled word will be displayed in the first box. In the above example the word accommodate is misspelled. To correct this, click on the correct spelling in the suggestions box and click Change. Sometimes there might

not be a spelling suggestion. In this case type the correct word in the first box and click Change. Sometimes the word might not be recognised by Word; if this is the case click on Ignore. There is also an option to add the word to the dictionary so that Word will recognise it in future.

5. The computer will display the message 'The spelling check is complete' when all the errors have been corrected. Click OK.

Summary

If the grammar and punctuation in a sentence is incorrect, the whole meaning can be distorted. This can result in the correct message not being delivered. Proofreading for spelling and grammar is a vital part of written communication. One-half of the communications module is focused on written communication and marks may be lost for poor grammar, incorrect use of punctuation and spelling mistakes.

Exercises

1. Pick out the nouns in the followings sentences:
    - Jack is eating a plum.
    - The watch is broken.
    - Jake painted a beautiful picture.
    - Thomas played the guitar.
    - Julie drove the tractor on the farm.

2. Pick out the adjectives in the following sentences:
    - Four cats climbed the tree.
    - Where is my blue jumper?
    - It is near the glass door.
    - What do you think of my new dress?
    - Dolly lives in a big house.

3. Pick out the adverbs in the following sentences:
    - I will visit Sean tomorrow.
    - Jack swam quickly in the pool.
    - Laura accidently broke the glass.
    - We will go to the pub soon.
    - I always lock the front door.

4. Pick out the pronouns in the following sentences:
    - She went to the park with Rover.
    - Six of us went in the small car.
    - I love watching them having fun.
    - We played with the dog and then we let her sleep.
    - Did you see the lovely picture I painted?

5. Pick out the prepositions in the following sentences:
    - John was studying in the library.

- The cat ran up the tree.
- Michael arrived before Mary.
- Anthony climbed onto the raft.
- Eileen was asleep during the lesson.

Learners will be able to:

- demonstrate an understanding of various non-verbal and visual codes
- demonstrate an awareness of ways in which the body communicates non- verbally
- demonstrate appropriate non-verbal communication in a range of settings
- recognise the role of perception in the communication process and factors that affect it
- construct and interpret visual aids and/or images
- recognise the ways we receive information from the physical environment, for example structure, shape, colour, texture, smell, sound.

Unit 3

Non-Verbal and Visual Communication

Non-Verbal and Visual Codes

Learning Outcomes

Learners will:

- understand how non-verbal and visual codes can add value in the communication process
- understand the various media we use to communicate non-verbally.

Introduction

Signs, symbols, images, cartoons, body signals, music, numbers, dance and colour are all forms of non-verbal and visual codes we use to communicate important messages. Non-verbal language and visual codes can be interpreted through any language, and as we are living in an age where visual stimuli are everywhere, it is important to consider how we can communicate our message and how we can add value by using a combination of the different media of communication to ensure that the message is reinforced.

Music

Music, as defined in *Collins Dictionary*, is an 'art form using a melodious and harmonious combination of notes'.

Music can add value in the communication process. The expression 'music to one's ears' is well known and means that the person receiving the message is very pleased to hear the information, as it means something pleasant or enjoyable. It is a pleasing sound created vocally and instrumentally. It has rhythm and melody and is appealing to human beings. It is a means of personal expression for the composer, and gives the recipient an opportunity to express themselves through the medium of music, be it song, tune or rhythm.

Good music in the life of a child provides many benefits. It promotes a positive attitude and encourages self-expression, self-esteem and creativity. Music takes a child into a whole new world of imagination: rhythm, rhyme and harmony.

Learning to play a musical instrument has lots of benefits. It sharpens the mind, teaches discipline and relieves stress.

Different types of music appeal to us at different stages of our lives. Music is often used to mark special events in people's lives and during these events, marriages or funerals for example, certain music will be played. Music can be symbolic and can add an extra medium of communication in church services, ceremonies, sporting events, films, advertisements and celebrations.

Music is an international language that crosses all barriers. It is one of the few ways in which people from different cultures can not only identify themselves but also communicate with each other and find common ground.

Using appropriate background music during a presentation can add flair and professionalism and make your presentation interesting. Adding music to certain segments of your presentation can engage your audience, and also break the monotony of a long presentation.

Music also has a role in business. The background music played in shops or stores can affect the way a customer behaves. There is a link between the tempo of music and the activity of customers in different settings. Jingles, which are original tunes composed specifically to support a certain brand, are widespread in advertising. They are effective in enhancing recall of the brand name and key selling points.

Noise

Any sound that is so loud that it interferes with the sending and receiving of a message is termed 'noise' in the context of communication theory. 'I can't hear a word that you are saying' usually means that the receiver cannot receive the message because of noise interference that is preventing the message being transmitted to them through the normal channels, because the noise is louder than the words.

Sound

We associate different sounds with different events. For example, we associate the sound of thunder with a storm, which in literature may reflect an atmosphere of anger or disquiet. We associate the sounds of birds singing on a sunny morning with summer, and happiness; it's hard to be sad when one wakes up to a beautiful day. We associate the sound of silence with one of two things: that people are so comfortable with each other they find words are not necessary; or that people in the group have fallen out and there is tension, so no one is talking. Sounds can frighten us, delight us or distract us. The following exercise might provide good openers for a personal story.

Exercise

Complete one of the following stories:

I was awakened from my sleep by the sound of someone moving in the bedroom. I was clutched by fear. My heart was racing at ninety to the dozen. I was in a state of panic and so paralysed that I couldn't move.

OR

He thought he had convinced me to accept the deal, but I was not happy. Something about it didn't add up. It sounded fishy to me.

OR

I was in a remote part of Donegal and woke to the sound of the cuckoo and the corncrake. It brought back memories of my child-hood, as these and other sounds of nature were a regular feature of the summers of my youth.

Dance

Dance, rhythm, movement and music are often interconnected in the communication process. They can communicate passionate, powerful messages. Dance and rhythm are associated with agility, energy, expression and movement. Dance is an arrangement of steps to a particular time and requires a range of body movements by the dancer. The beat of the music should keep pace with the rhythm of the dance.

We also associate this form of communication with being entertained. The show *Riverdance*, for example, successfully combined traditional song, music and dance to produce something that became internationally renowned. It has been turned into a multi-million euro industry.

Rhythm

We respond to rhythm; it makes us want to dance and express ourselves to the beat of the music. Rhythm appeals to our emotions and it can have a powerful influence on how we communicate.

Poetry is often called the music of the soul and it appeals to our aesthetic self. Choreography is the arrangement of steps and movement for dancing. Movement is the interlinking of expression to produce the overall communication.

The dance can't be communicated without the dancer.

The rhythm can't be communicated without the music.

The music can't be communicated without the musician.

The musician can't communicate without the tune.

The tune can't be communicated without a composer who communicates it through a unique arrangement of notes.

Colour

Colour is a visual sensation, it stimulates the brain. Colour is a non-verbal method of communication, and specific colours are associated with certain meanings; for example; red for danger, blue and green represent peace and tranquility, and orange emits warmth and energy.

Colour plays an important role in business. It is used to convey a marketing message, and is an important part of the company's identity. Take the Google logo as an example; the colour of the logo makes it instantly recognisable. The blue used in the IBM logo represents security and reliability. It makes a statement about the company's expertise, reinforcing its strength in the industry. It is a great example of a simple yet powerful emblem.

We express ourselves in many ways through colour; for example how we dress, the colours in our homes and gardens. When we dress we select the colours that express how we feel. We also dress to suit an occasion; black for a funeral rather than brightly coloured clothes. When we decorate our homes, we pick colours to surround us based on how we want to feel in that environment.

The combination of colour and numbers can reinforce a message even more, for example the colours of medals for first, second and third.

Exercise

How can colour add value to the way you communicate your message?

Symbols

Symbols are used throughout the world to communicate the same message regardless of what language is used in any particular country.

The dollar ($) is the official currency of many countries. The euro (€) is the basic unit of currency in Europe. Many times we need to convert one into the other to value one against the other.

We use the symbols + − x ÷ to add, subtract, multiply and divide. An arrow points us in a particular direction. All these symbols are part of a global language.

Logos and trademarks

These are symbols associated with companies and other organisations. They are used to differentiate companies from their competitors.

A visual logo can express something faster than written words. Signs and symbols can cross international language barriers.

Exercise

Think of a logo you are familiar with and discuss how it adds value to the marketing of the product.

Numbers

The *Penguin English Dictionary* defines a number as a 'word, numeral, digit or other symbol that is used in counting or calculating quantities and in referring to things by their position in a series'. We use numbers to communicate important messages every day of our lives. As these numbers are relevant to our needs, we are careful to make sure they represent the true situation or value of the item being purchased. We are also careful to make sure we get the correct change and we count it in numbers and symbols (€1.20 is counted as one euro and twenty cents).

However, if the numbers have no relevance to us, we switch off. When presenting information, it is important to use numbers sparingly and wisely. The onus is on you to present numbers in a clear and understandable way. Decide on the numbers that are most relevant to the audience's needs and present them so that they can be clearly understood and remembered.

Theme and repetition are helpful in remembering numbers. Use comparisons to support your numbers. You could also use visual aids or even gestures. Numbers can add to or detract from the message depending on how you use them. It might be worth remembering this if you are giving a technical presentation.

Numbers have many advantages in real life.

- They provide quantifiable evidence.
- They record days, months, years that we spend on earth.
- They allow people to research their ancestral roots.
- They give us the opportunity to compare and contrast.

- We use numbers to put a monetary value on wages and to pay our bills.
- We check our lotto numbers and hope we can declare ourselves millionaires.
- Time, money, climate, population and distance are all measured using numbers.

Numbers are important in the world of sport. Competitors, players, horses, etc. are all identified by numbers, so that we can recognise them easier and faster.

Look at the these two images and discuss how numbers play a part in each sport.

Months of the Year

30 days hath September
April, June and November,
All the rest have 31,

February has but 28,
Except in leap year once in 4
When February has 1 day more.

The following is a recipe for disaster because without measurements, which require numbers, the recipe cannot be followed.

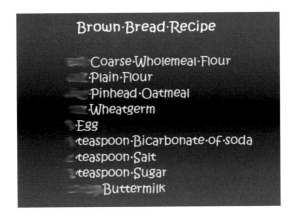

Brown·Bread·Recipe

Coarse·Wholemeal·Flour
·Plain·Flour
Pinhead·Oatmeal
Wheatgerm
·Egg
teaspoon·Bicarbonate·of·soda
teaspoon·Salt
teaspoon·Sugar
Buttermilk

Without numbers the message is lost in this situation!

Recipes rely on numbers to provide the quantities of particular ingredients which need to be mixed in a certain proportion and in a particular sequence to produce the intended result. This mixture is then placed in a specifically sized dish and cooked at a precise temperature for a determined amount of time to produce the end product. Recipes need numbers so that we know what quantities of ingredients to use, and the temperature and time taken to produce the desired results.

Numbers are important in setting goals. Using the SMART goal template, notice how vital it is to have quantifiable evidence in order to be able to set a clear goal. Goal setting, like so much else, is a numbers game.

SMART goal template

1. Specific: A general statement is not sufficient. For example, if I say I want to earn more money, that is not a goal as it is too general and it could be interpreted as wishful thinking. If I set a goal to earn an extra €5,000 per year, then I know exactly what I have to achieve. Now I can put a measure on it.
2. Measurable: How much? By when? For example, €100 per week?
3. Attainable: What do I need to do differently to achieve it? Work an extra ten hours a week or take on a different job?
4. Reward: Get to save for that Australian holiday.
5. Time: One year.

You will set goals each time you start a new module. The SMART goal template is a good way to set your goal and decide 'how much' and 'by when'.

Changing money to a different currency is a great example of how we use a variety of different non-verbal and visual codes at the same time. We use numbers, images of each country's flag, codes for each country or currency (for example EUR), and we use mathematical symbols to calculate the exchange rate. All of these codes can be understood by people of any nationality across the world.

Codes

A code is a set of letters, symbols, colours, etc. that allows information to be communicated briefly. A code is also a set of guidelines designed to set out acceptable behaviour. There are many different types of code: letters, symbols, numbers, colours, or a combination of these allows people to identify, for example, an article of interest or a course on offer in a college handbook.

Code of behaviour: A code can be a set of guidelines designed to set out acceptable behaviour based on the values of an organisation.

Code of ethics: A code that governs the principles of conduct for an individual or group.

Dress code: The type of clothes that are acceptable and that reflect the ethos of a company.

Colour code: A system of colours that convey a particular meaning. The Safe Pass code, for example, enables information to be communicated clearly as each colour conveys a distinct meaning.

PIN code: Four numbers that allow us to access our bank accounts. As it is a secret combination of numbers only you can use it, unless you allow others to access it.

The Forest Code shown below sets out the standard of behaviour expected from people using the forest for recreation.

The Forest Code

- Please take nothing but photographs and leave nothing but footprints.
- Please bring all litter home.
- Leave the wild flowers and shrubs for others to enjoy.
- Do not disturb the wildlife.
- Dogs to be kept on a leash in the interest of safety.
- The lighting of fires is prohibited.
- Young children should be supervised.

Exercise

In pairs, come up with a suitable code for your organisation/club, taking into account the ethos of the organisation/club, etc.

Summary

Non-verbal and visual codes are an important part of communication. They condense the message and through the use of signs, symbols, logos, numbers etc. they communicate accurate information at a glance. These visual and non-verbal codes can cross all international languages and they are instantly recognisable.

SECTION 2

Body Language

Learning Outcomes

Learners will:

- have an awareness of ways in which we communicate non-verbally using our bodies.

Introduction

The human body is capable of producing over 700,000 different movements (Hartland and Tosh, 2001). From the moment of our birth to the time of our death we communicate through our body language. We also respond to the body language of others in a positive or negative way. This in turn creates more thoughts and feelings; our body language is the outward manifestation of these. It is an ongoing communication process and continues until our last breath when we become still and silent.

Body language helps communicate our attitudes. We convert our attitudes into assertive, aggressive or passive behaviour. The gestures we use give the person observing our body language clues to the type of person we are. Therefore, our gestures, our posture, our facial expression, our eye contact and the personal space we maintain all make up the way we communicate.

Facial expressions

Facial expressions are often the outward signs of our emotional state. We can instantly recognise what kind of day someone is having from the look on their face. Most of our expressions are born out of the four primary feelings: sad, mad, glad and scared. The different levels of intensity in the feelings we express are often very clear in our facial expressions. How often have we heard it said, 'I knew by her face that something was wrong?'

Gesture

Hand gestures are another great form of expression.

- Victory (hands in the air).
- Sealing the deal (handshake).
- Comparison ('on the one hand... on the other hand').
- Get out of my way (hand pushing someone).
- Encouraging (patting someone on the back).

Posture

- Standing tall (confidence).
- Slumping (nervous/bored).
- Smooth movements (in control).
- Eye contact (connection).
- Personal space (safety/comfort).

Exercises

1. Examine each picture below and explain what the picture means when converted into human behaviour.

2. How would you use body language to display the meaning of the following?

Crocodile tears

Grinning like a Cheshire cat

Sounds fishy to me

Giving me the cold shoulder

The eye of an eagle

A fish out of water

Bull in a china shop

As lucky as a black cat

A bear with a sore head

Like the cat that got the cream

As cute as a fox

He blew a fuse

Body language can communicate louder than words. Intuitively, we sometimes get a sense that someone is being insincere, uncomfortable, putting you off or in a bad mood. Not looking someone in the eye can lead to doubt about the person or what they are saying. Personal space is very important; if your personal space is violated you feel threatened.

Signals

We give non-verbal signals by our actions and gestures, for example boredom, insecurity, anger, frustration, jealousy and tiredness. A baby communicates in signals before it ever utters a word. This highlights the importance of body language; if we could not interpret body language, we could not respond in the appropriate way. When a baby gets sick and needs attention there are a whole series of messages sent through body language: crying, listlessness, lethargy, rise in body temperature, rapid breathing and possibly screaming depending on the child's level of pain.

Proximity

Proximity is defined in the *Penguin English Dictionary* as 'nearness in space, time or association'. Proximity can communicate important messages. How near you are to another person can be interpreted as an association with the other person.

When teenagers are asserting their independence it can be detrimental for them to be seen with old fogies who might tarnish their reputation with their peer group. Close proximity is often evident at the start of a match when the team huddle around each other, showing unity of purpose by their body language and closeness. When their team wins, the fans want to get as close as possible to their heroes because they have an emotional attachment to them. The tribal instinct is yearning to be expressed by being identified with the team and getting as close to them as possible.

In a conflict situation, people sometimes give away their power because they become angry and blame the other person rather than dealing with the issue that is causing them the problem. A lady once told the story that another person was invading her personal space at work on a continuous basis. One day, she lost her temper with the other person, but as soon as she did she realised that she had given away her power.

Orientation

When we are in a familiar place and with familiar people we are orientated and our body language sends out a signal that we are calm and secure. If we are in an unfamiliar place we are suspicious, alert to danger and can feel threatened, unsure of what to expect. Sometimes in these surroundings we feel disorientated and our body language can signal our insecurity and sense of feeling lost.

Orientation involves being able to adjust and find your bearings in unfamiliar surroundings. It means adjusting to a new set of circumstances and getting to know the rules and values of an organisation through face-to-face interaction with people who are established members. This will make the transition easier and will help one connect and be orientated in an agreeable way.

Mime

Charlie Chaplin is a great example of a comic actor from the silent film era who communicated largely through his body language. He was the master of mime. His expressions, movement, his pauses, his stillness, his use of space, his creativity and exaggerated movements enabled his audience to receive his message loud and clear. He entertained millions through the use of gestures, facial expression, props and body language.

Mime is a great way of showing how effective gesture and body movement can be in communicating a message without the use of words.

Exercise

Act out your favourite advertisement on TV without using words.

How we communicate when speaking

Actions speak louder than words. This diagram shows us just how loud. When we communicate a message, our body language does over half the talking (Mehrabian, 2008).

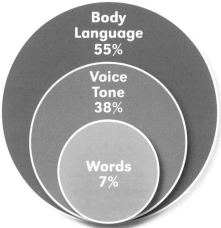

However, it is the whole package that makes the impact, and it can be difficult to separate the three components in a given situation. You never get a second chance to make a first impression and there are times when that first impression is vital, especially in a job interview.

It is always important to smile. A smile is a facial expression that communicates friendliness, pleasure, amusement, satisfaction and encouragement.

> *'Man is the only animal that blushes, or needs to.'*
>
> (Mark Twain)

> *'There is sacredness in tears; they are not a mark of*
> *weakness, but of power.*
> *They speak more eloquently than ten thousand tongues.*
> *They are messengers of overwhelming grief ...*
> *and unspeakable love.'*
>
> (Washington Irving)

> *'The eyes have one language everywhere.'*
>
> (George Herbert)

Summary

Body language is a large part of how we communicate. Understanding that our attitudes and our gestures convert into important messages should make us realise why body language communicates a lot louder than words.

The Value of a Smile

It costs nothing, but creates much.

It enriches those who receive, without impoverishing those who give.

It happens in a flash and the memory of it sometimes lasts forever.

None are so rich they can get along without it and none so poor but are richer for its benefits.

It creates happiness in the home, fosters good will in a business, and is the countersign of friends.

It is the rest to the weary, daylight to the discouraged, sunshine to the sad, and nature's best antidote for trouble.

Yet it cannot be taught, begged, borrowed or stolen, for it is something that is no earthly good to anyone until it is given away.

And if in life's mad rush, should people be too tired to give you a smile, may we ask you to leave one of yours?

For nobody needs a smile so much as those who have none left to give!

Exercise

Below is a list of general non-verbal behaviours. Try to give two or three meanings to each behaviour.

1. A person nods his head up and down.
2. A person's lower lip quivers slightly.
3. A person smiles slightly.
4. A person yawns.
5. A person shrugs her shoulders.
6. A person inhales quickly.
7. A person sighs loudly.
8. A person grins.
9. A person avoids eye contact.
10. A person crosses her arms.

Perception in Communication

Learning Outcomes

Learners will:
- recognise the role of perception in the communication process and factors that affect it, such as prejudice, discrimination and stereotyping.

Introduction

We all perceive information through the senses. Problems arise when we have preconceived ideas about a situation or a person and, as a result, we have formed our opinions prior to getting the knowledge or experience that is required to make an informed judgement.

These preconceived ideas can often lead to prejudice and can cause us to judge people unfairly. This may lead to distrust and bias. If there are no drastic consequences, it is just a misjudgement, but if our prejudice is rooted in hatred and fear, it can lead to segregation, violence, war and death. The Rosa Lee Parks story demonstrates how prejudice led to black people being regarded as second-class citizens in the USA and having their rights violated as a result.

Exercise

Read the following extract and comment on the impact the story had on you. Have our attitudes changed in today's society?

Rosa Lee Parks 1913 - 2005

"I knew someone had to take the first step and I made up my mind not to move"

Rosa Parks sitting on a Montgomery, Alabama bus in late December 1956 after the American Supreme Court outlawed segregation on buses

Most historians date the beginning of the modern civil rights movement in the USA to 1st December 1955. According to legend, on that day, a weary black woman in Montgomery, Alabama, sat in the 'for whites only' front section of a bus. What really happened is as follows: Rosa Parks left Montgomery Fair, the department store where she did repairs on men's clothing, as usual. It was true that she was tired after work, and pain in her shoulders, back and neck was troubling her. By chance the bus driver happened to be the very man who had forced her off the bus back in 1943. She did not, as myth would have it, sit in the whites-only front part, but beside a black man at the back. As more white people got on, the driver told her to give up her seat. She refused. *'If you don't stand up, I'm going to call the police,'* he threatened. To which she replied: *'You may do that.'* Arrested, found guilty of violating the segregation law and fined, she consulted her husband and her mother and decided that her arrest would serve as a test case.

Mrs. Parks' lonely act of defiance began a movement that ended legal segregation in America, and made her an inspiration to freedom-loving people everywhere.

Nearly all Montgomery's black citizens participated in the resulting boycott, which lasted for 381 days.

Almost 100 people were arrested including Parks and the young Martin Luther King. On 20th December 1956, just over a year later, the Supreme Court supported the decision of a lower court, and federal injunctions were served on the bus company officials to end segregation. Montgomery's buses were integrated on 21st December, 1956.

Her act of civil disobedience, what seems a simple gesture of defiance many years later, was in fact a dangerous, even reckless move in 1950s Alabama. In refusing to move, she risked legal sanction and perhaps even physical harm, but she also set in motion something far beyond the control of the city authorities. Mrs. Parks clarified for people far beyond Montgomery the cruelty and humiliation inherent in the laws and customs of segregation.

That moment on the Cleveland Avenue bus also turned a very private woman into a reluctant symbol and torchbearer in the quest for racial equality and of a movement that became increasingly organised and sophisticated in making demands and getting results.

'She sat down in order that we might stand up', the Rev. Jesse Jackson said on the day she died. He went on to say *'Paradoxically, her imprisonment opened the doors for our long journey to freedom.'*

In 1957, Rosa Parks moved to Detroit, Michigan where she served on the staff of US Democratic Congressman, John Conyers, until her retirement in 1988.

She continued to be extremely active, travelling extensively to lecture on the civil rights movement and the social and economic problems that continued to plague black Americans. In 1987 Rosa Park founded the Rosa and Raymond Parks Institute for Self-Development, which aims to help young people and educate them about civil rights.

President Clinton presented Mrs. Parks with the Presidential Medal of Freedom in 1996. In 1999 she was awarded America's highest civilian honour, the Congressional Gold Medal. After her death her casket was placed in the rotunda of the United States Capitol for two days, so that the nation could pay its respects to the woman whose courage changed the lives of so many. She was the first woman in American history to lie in state at the Capitol, an honour usually reserved for Presidents of the United States.

4

Prejudice

Under the Equality Status Act 2000, people cannot be discriminated against because of their gender, civil status, family status, age, disability, race, sexual orientation, religious beliefs, or membership of the traveller community. This legislation now exists to protect the interests of groups of people who have been discriminated against historically. Today also it is important for us to understand how we can adapt our communication to ensure that people who are visually, mobility or hearing impaired can receive our message.

Most people with disabilities involving vision, hearing or mobility can become discouraged because people without disabilities have inadequate information about their needs. We must have the necessary confidence to learn to communicate in new ways. Learning an extra skill such as sign language, or simply considering others' needs, will help to break down barriers between people in society.

EXAMPLE

Speaking one to one with someone who is hearing impaired.

It is important when speaking to a person with a hearing impairment that you use the medium that will allow them to interpret the message with ease. The following guidelines may help to overcome some of the incorrect information about communicating with a person with a hearing disability.

Another effective means of communication with a person who has a hearing disability is through the use of sign language. These signs represent the letters of the alphabet, allowing you to sign words. Your body language allows the recipient to feel the intensity and sincerity of the message.

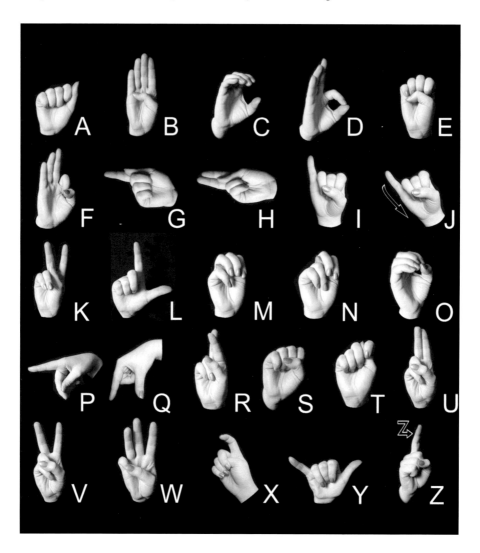

Stereotyping

Stereotyping is another way we categorise people without knowing the relevant facts.

What colours our view?

The more diverse nature is the more we say 'wow,' except in the case of our fellow human beings. With the right attitude you should be willing to explore all situations and judge all situations and people on their own merits. We often perceive a situation through what we see and hear. Because these three children have green hats with shamrocks on them, we might assume that they are all Irish. This may be true or false, but until you get the facts, it is only an opinion. Take the test below. (Correct answers are at the end of this section.)

From left to right, fill in what you think might be the answers to these questions for children A, B and C above.

	Child A	Child B	Child C
Nationality			
Age			
Location			
Favourite school subject			
Favourite hobby			
Special skill			

Remember, in living our lives and communicating with each other, our perception of reality is less important than reality itself.

Summary

Our perceptions often influence how we think and how we behave. Pre-judging people without the facts can cause us to make wrong decisions that can have far-reaching consequences.

'Don't change the world, change the prescription of your glasses.'
(Swami Muktananda, master of meditation)

Answers (not the real answers, but they could be!)

	Child A	Child B	Child C
Nationality	Irish	Australian	Irish
Age	7	7	6
Location	Sydney	Sydney	Sydney
Favourite school subject	Maths	English	French
Favourite hobby	Football	Helping to cook	Climbing trees
Special skills	Whistling	Handstands	Magic tricks

Visual Aids

Introduction

We live in a visual age. We are constantly exposed to visual stimuli through the use of advertisements, TV, cinema, photography, etc. We find it difficult to take the message in without the visual stimulus.

We remember 30 per cent of what we see and hear. Visuals help us to keep focused on the message. Consequently, visual aids can be powerful tools in reinforcing our message.

PowerPoint

Microsoft PowerPoint is a popular visual aid that can enhance your presentation. However, it is important not to rely on PowerPoint as a 'crutch,' as your presentation may become boring. Slides should be kept clear, concise and easy to understand.

Remember, if you want to get your point across effectively, you must be passionate and enthusiastic about what you are saying. PowerPoint is only an aid.

PowerPoint Presentation

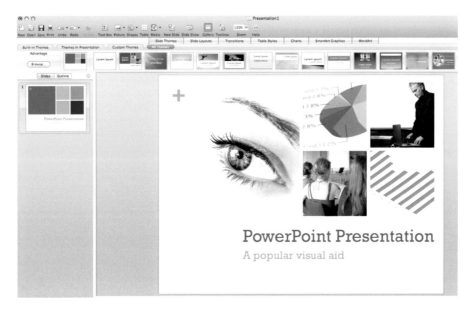

The poster

The poster is another visual aid that can help convey your message to your audience. An effective poster will enhance any presentation. Therefore, the design of the poster is very important. The first step in designing a poster is to address these questions.

- What message do you want to send?
- What do you want the receiver to think/do?
- What outcome do you want to achieve?
- How can visuals add to the message?

Tips for designing a poster

Plan your layout carefully.

- Plan headings and subheadings.

- Organise the information into sections.
- Aim for balance and simplicity.
- Decide where you want to add graphics, photographs, etc.
- Less is more – try not to present too much detail.
- Leave enough white space – the poster should have a clean, simple and uncluttered layout.
- Provide name and contact details.
- The information should flow (viewing sequence) by column or by row.

Choose colours that complement each other. Certain colours, certain yellows for example, are difficult to see and read. Text and background colours should sit well together. Make sure your foreground colour (text) is clear and easy on the eyes when combined with the background colour.

Font choice and size are very important when designing a poster. They will determine whether your audience will be able to read your poster with ease. If they can't, all your hard work will have been for nothing, so choose a font that is easy to read.

Graphics, photographs, diagrams, etc. are very important components of your poster. They will add interesting visuals, helping you to get your message across. Don't add unnecessary visuals as this will clutter your poster and make it too 'busy'. If necessary, enlarge and crop your visuals by zooming into the relevant part of the picture/visual. Make sure that any visuals are clear and of good quality. There are different ways to do this, depending on whether the visual is a graphic, photograph, diagram, etc.

Exercise

Which of the following two posters will have a better outcome? Why?

MISSING DOG

Black and white dog
missing since
Friday 2nd June
Please phone:
087 0000000

Have you seen Betsy?

Please help us to find Betsy.
She is a treasured family pet.

She was last seen outside our home
on Greenhill Road, Wicklow Town
on Friday 2nd June.

Reward offered.
If you have seen Betsy or have any information,
please phone John on

087 0000000

The above examples demonstrate the importance of a well-designed poster. The first poster gives only the basic information and does not interest the reader. The second poster instantly catches the eye with a picture of the missing dog. The personal language, clear, concise information and neat layout all add to the effectiveness of the second poster.

Use one of the following images, or any other image that appeals to you, to create a poster or a card for a particular occasion.

Summary

Visual stimuli add value to communication. We retain 10 per cent of what we hear and 30 per cent of what we see and hear.

SECTION 5
The Physical Environment

Learning Outcomes

Learners will:

- be able to identify the way we respond to the physical environment.

Introduction

We are constantly receiving messages from the physical environment. We receive messages through the weather: hot, cold, miserable, dreary, wet and damp; and through structure, sound, shape, colour and texture.

Each season has its own message

We get information from the physical environment through structure, shape, colour, texture, smell and sound. Nature gives us information through all these mediums on an ongoing basis. Each season brings its own unique colours, smells, shapes, sizes, textures and sounds.

The winter is usually bleak and dreary, with grey skies and little sunlight. The trees are bare and the weather is often dismal. This indicates a rest period for nature; food is scarce and the landscape is stark and bleak, with little colour. Natural light is in short supply and the dark of night falls quickly.

Sometimes there is a snowfall and this creates an entirely different atmosphere. The texture and temperature of the snow is a new experience. It allows children to make snowmen of all different shapes and sizes. The whole landscape is transformed into a winter wonderland through the whiteness of the snow and the glistening of the frost.

The physical environment changes in spring. The days are brighter, flowers begin to grow, the trees begin to bud and blossom. The sounds of nature are different; now the birds are singing. There are different textures; there is a different feel to the trees and flowers as they blossom and bloom.

The summer months express a different message again. We hear sounds that are not available to us at any other time of the year, like the cuckoo's song. Nature is in full bloom. Colour is in abundance. The weather is warm and sunny.

Autumn inspires different emotions. Trees are laden with fruit and berries, ripe for picking. The summer sun has ripened the fruit and it is now mellow and sweet and ready to be eaten. The crops from the fields are ready for harvesting. The weather is getting a little cooler and the days are getting a little shorter. The autumn colours are beginning to unfold and there is a sense that winter is just around the corner.

So the cycle continues as each season evokes different emotions, movements, scents, colours, sounds, tastes, textures and shapes.

Exercises

1. Using your sense of touch, describe the feeling of sandy soil and of boggy soil.

2. Think about how your responses are shaped by the physical environment through structure, shape, colour, texture, smell and sound. Comment on how it might be different, depending on whether you are at the seaside on a sunny summer's day, or on the top of a mountain on a cold bleak winter's evening.

Taking poetic inspiration from our physical environment

Eoghan O'Sullivan, a 2010 Leaving Certificate student at Salesian College, Celbridge, has compiled the following account of how we and the physical environment are constantly in communication. He took four poets from the Leaving Certificate syllabus and looked at how they were inspired by nature.

Our physical surroundings are constantly communicating with us, frequently in ways that we overlook or fail to recognise. Yet, in spite of this, we do receive its messages. We make use of the information it provides, often without fully realising how we have gained it, or even what the method of communication was. For us, the receipt of this knowledge is a process of which we are mostly unaware.

Poets, however, are more finely tuned to these messages than the rest of us, and many have been greatly inspired by their surroundings. They have been moved to write works of great beauty, works which capture exactly how they viewed a place, and which express the poets' state of mind at the time. The poets' mood affects how they viewed the scene before them. If they were sad, lonely or angry they are more likely to write a darker poem than they might otherwise have done, describing what they see in a more negative way. Communication with our physical environment is hugely affected by our own moods and emotions.

In a way, the message we receive holds a mirror up to our own feelings. If we're in a bad mood then it's very unlikely that we will find anything positive in our surroundings. An example of this would be two people looking at a tree in the middle of autumn, just as the leaves are changing colour. One person could look at the tree and see how it is dying after the summer. They feel the changing of the seasons and know that the long, dark winter is coming. In contrast with this, another person might see the loveliness of the tree's autumn colours, and be amazed by its beauty.

In this piece I intend to discuss four different poems, with the aim of showing how these poems were inspired by various physical environments, and that they were all inspired in different ways.

The first poem that I will deal with is W. B. Yeats's 'The Wild Swans at Coole.'

The Wild Swans at Coole

The trees are in their autumn beauty,
The woodland paths are dry,
Under the October twilight the water
Mirrors a still sky;
Upon the brimming water among the stones
Are nine and fifty swans.

The nineteenth autumn has come upon me
Since I first made my count;
I saw, before I had well finished,

All suddenly mount
And scatter wheeling in great broken rings
Upon their clamorous wings.

I have looked upon those brilliant creatures,
And now my heart is sore.
All's changed since I, hearing at twilight,
The first time on this shore,
The bell-beat of their wings above my head,
Trod with a lighter tread.

Unwearied still, lover by lover,
They paddle in the cold,
Companionable streams or climb the air;
Their hearts have not grown old;
Passion or conquest, wander where they will,
Attend upon them still.

But now they drift on the still water
Mysterious, beautiful;
Among what rushes will they build,

By what lake's edge or pool
Delight men's eyes, when I awake some day
To find they have flown away?

This poem was inspired by the scenic Coole Lake in the west of Ireland, an area which is known for its spectacular natural beauty. Yet, in spite of the appeal of his environment, Yeats is acutely aware of his own misery. He describes the beauty which inspired him to write, but it is tinged with an undertone of his own sadness. He is lonely and feels the burden of his increasing age, and everything he sees reminds him of this: the trees shedding their leaves, the October evening fading into winter, the twilit sky darkening as night approaches. Even the number of swans (fifty-nine) potentially has a negative aspect for Yeats. This is because swans are creatures that mate for life, and the odd number of swans present may mean that there is one which does not have a partner. These are the ideas that Yeats was absorbing from his surroundings, and the poet's experience shows the volume of information that we can gain from our environment.

It cannot be denied that the poem creates a pleasing image in our minds, but there is an ever-present sense of sorrow also. Once again, this is an example of how the mood of the observer affects the message they receive from their physical surroundings.

Another effect the setting has on Yeats is that it reminds him of the last time he was by this lake. Several things trigger memories within him, memories that he might otherwise have forgotten. Communications from our physical environment regularly have this kind of impact on people. I would imagine that it has happened to almost everyone; a sound, a smell, or even the sight of something brings back memories that hadn't been thought of for years.

The main trigger in this case is the sound of the swan's wings beating as they fly. This sound inspires him to recall his youth. Nineteen years before, he stood on the shore and counted the swans as well; on that occasion the sound of their wings and their natural magnificence improved his mood, allowed him to feel happier within himself. This is another effect that our environment can have on us. The splendour of physical settings can always be relied upon to improve our mood and to help us forget our troubles.

A final message that Yeats takes from his lakeside environment is to do with the timelessness of nature and how the natural world moves without us. He realises that although nineteen years have passed, he would not be able to tell the group of swans he sees today from the group that he saw then. He can look at them and convince himself that it is the same group and that the passage of time hasn't affected them at all. Again, his surroundings are influencing his state of mind.

The poet also realises that in some ways mankind is largely powerless. It occurs to him that the swans could easily fly away tomorrow, leaving the lake forever, and he would be helpless to stop this from happening. Even though their presence brings him joy and peace of mind, he has no control over them, and could do nothing to stop them leaving if they wished. It is not unusual for people to receive insights such as this from their physical surroundings.

The second poem I will discuss is again by an Irish poet. This poem is 'Canal Bank Walk' and is one of Patrick Kavanagh's most famous works.

Canal Bank Walk

> Leafy-with-love banks and the green waters of the canal
> Pouring redemption for me, that I do
> The will of God, wallow in the habitual, the banal,
> Grow with nature again as before I grew.
> The bright stick trapped, the breeze adding a third
> Party to the couple kissing on an old seat,
> And a bird gathering materials for the nest for the Word
> Eloquently new and abandoned to its delirious beat.
> O unworn world enrapture me, encapture me in a web
> Of fabulous grass and eternal voices by a beech,
> Feed the gaping need of my senses, give me ad lib
> To pray unselfconsciously with overflowing speech
> For this soul needs to be honoured with a new dress woven
> From green and blue things and arguments that cannot be proven.

This poem was inspired by Dublin's Grand Canal, especially the area around Baggot Street Bridge. In 1955 (the year this poem was written), Kavanagh was recovering from illness and spent many hours resting and writing poetry on the banks of the canal.

From the opening lines of this poem it is clear that his recent recovery from cancer has filled Kavanagh with optimism, as well as with a desire to appreciate the world around him. It would be difficult for him to be any more positive

about the environment in which he finds himself. Everything is wonderful. He wants to celebrate every aspect of the beauty that he sees: the leafy banks, the green water, the couple near by. Kavanagh's enthusiasm is so great that he wants to honour everything of the scene before him which others might find unremarkable. He is overflowing in his eagerness.

It is clear that Kavanagh was receiving a deeply inspiring message from his surroundings; they are doing nothing but giving him joy. His attitude while writing 'Canal Bank Walk' is obviously very different from the attitude that Yeats had as he wrote 'The Wild Swans at Coole.' As a result, the tones of both poems are poles apart. Yeats was looking inward, focusing on his own sadness, his environment constantly reminding him of his own misery. By contrast, Kavanagh was looking outwards, focused on the wonders of the world around him and uplifted by his environment. Once again, this shows how our individual mindsets change the way our surroundings communicate with us. More importantly, it shows how dealing with our surroundings in a positive way is infinitely more rewarding.

The power of Kavanagh's surroundings is such that he feels he can almost sense some divine machinery guiding and overseeing the natural processes he sees; everything has its own place and function in the world. Even a bird building its nest is serving some higher purpose.

He also realises, due to messages from his environment, that as a result of his illness the world is once again renewed. His new-found enthusiasm means that he can look at everything with fresh eyes and focus on the beauty he sees, without cynicism or bitterness. He realises that to do otherwise would be a waste of time, and so he wants to appreciate as much beauty as he can, to make the most of the chance that he has been given. This shows how our physical surroundings can sometimes inspire us to alter our habits and outlook on life. Kavanagh's epiphany means that he has a better outlook on life, which will more than likely make him a better person from this moment on.

The final insight Kavanagh receives in the course of this poem is that it can be better for the mental well-being of a person to sometimes simply accept the splendour of what they see and to value it for what it is, without always feeling the need to further explain, clarify or understand it. He feels that such analysis can somehow cheapen what we were admiring, as we can forget exactly why we wanted to understand it in the first place.In such ways do our physical surroundings inspire deep and meaningful insights.

The next poem I will discuss is one by Derek Walcott, a poet from the Caribbean island of St Lucia.

Pentecost

Better a jungle in the head
than rootless concrete.
Better to stand bewildered
by the fireflies' crooked street;

winter lamps do not show
where the sidewalk is lost,
nor can these tongues of snow
speak for the Holy Ghost;

the self-increasing silence
of words dropped from a roof
points along iron railings,
direction, in not proof.

But best is this night surf
with slow scriptures of sand,

that sends, not quite a seraph,
but a late cormorant,

whose fading cry propels
through phosphorescent shoal
what, in my childhood gospels,
used to be called the Soul.

This poem was inspired by the landscape of a North American city, most likely Boston or New York. In spite of Walcott's Caribbean origins, he spent much of his adult life working in various US cities, places where he never felt truly at home.

Here the grey, concreted landscape of this unknown American city awakens homesickness within him; he hates the dull, urban landscape of the city and is pining for the vibrant, lush world of his island home.

The message that his environment is giving him evokes memories of his native land: the jungle, the fireflies. This is similar to how Yeats's surroundings in 'The Wild Swans at Coole' caused him to remember his past, but here Walcott is not only remembering a happier time in his life, he is also remembering a happier place. This is another common effect that our physical setting can have on us; quite often it can cause us to wish that we were somewhere else, be it somewhere cleaner, somewhere calmer, or somewhere where we felt less stressed.

This poem is different from the others I have discussed in that it deals with two distinct physical landscapes, both of which had a part in how the poem was formed. While it is true that the city's landscape provided the primary catalyst for the poem's creation, it is the landscape of St Lucia that relieves the poet's stress, even the thought of it allows him to feel calmer. This is a crucial factor in maintaining the poem's general air of serenity throughout.

Walcott's main problems with the city are to do with its unnatural origin, and his difficulty in finding any divine presence in it. The lack of nature's presence is something he cannot handle, coming as he does from an island where close contact with nature is an integral part of day-to-day existence. The communication that the city (his physical environment) is having with Walcott is one which feels cold, sterile and closed off. It is simply not what he's used to.

For Walcott, the city feels empty. It seems likely that he is the type of person who seeks out the divine in nature and now that his contact with nature is gone, his connection to the divine has been severed. This is deeply distressing for him.

People can often become uncomfortable when they are removed from the physical environment to which they are accustomed; they often find it difficult to settle, to relax. The effects that our surroundings have upon us are not always positive.

However, in the final section of this poem, Walcott grows more calm. His memories of St Lucia fill him with contentment and help him block out the city before him. Their beauty gives him strength to carry on, to bear spending more time in this city. Many people engage in similar activities. In times of stress they retreat to a mental sanctuary, a place which helps them block out the world and fills them with tranquility. It allows them to overcome difficult situations and to persevere in their daily lives. It is interesting to note how even the memory of a physical landscape can have a positive effect upon our state of mind.

The final poem I will discuss is one by an American poet. The poet's name is T.S. Eliot and the poem is the third from a series of poems called 'Landscapes.'

Usk

Do not suddenly break the branch, or
Hope to find
The white hart behind the white well.
Glance aside, not for lance, do not spell
Old enchantments. Let them sleep.
'Gently dip, but not too deep,'
Lift your eyes
Where the roads dip and where the roads rise
Seek only there
Where the grey light meets the green air
The hermit's chapel, the pilgrim's prayer.

This poem was inspired by the village of Usk in Wales. Out of all the poems that I have discussed so far, this is probably the one which is most difficult to interpret, but I feel that it should still be included, even if only on the merits of its poetic artistry. As with all poetry, we do not need to fully understand it in its entirety to appreciate its beauty. We can, and should, simply enjoy it for what it is.

From the beginning of this poem to its end, there is a powerful sense of peace and awe permeating every line. The poet is content simply sitting and admiring the landscape before him. The message it is giving him, or so he feels, is that there is no need to invade this landscape to appreciate it; there is no need to seek to fully understand it, or to take away trophies (i.e. branches) from the setting to be displayed at a later date. It should be enough to simply have been there, without feeling the need to destroy something for self-gratification. This is yet another example of the type of insight that people can receive from their physical surroundings.

Another aspect of the physical environment here is the region's history, be it legendary history or otherwise. This is not something that we have encountered in the other works discussed, but it is an important facet of how our setting sends us messages, how it becomes meaningful to us. Think of the number of fields or rocks that are famous because of the events that occurred there, and of the number of people that visit these places to see them. It is clear that having an understanding of the history present in the landscape allows us to communicate with it and to understand it on a whole new level.

In the case of Usk, history is the mythical legend of King Arthur. These fantastic legends of knights and ladies have been heard by millions of people worldwide, and have brought joy to many. Eliot ponders this as he sits observing the scenery before him.

But, like Kavanagh in 'Canal Bank Walk', this poem draws to a close with an epiphany, once again as a result of a communication from the poet's physical environment. Suddenly he decides to dismiss these old legends from his mind: 'Let them sleep.' This about face is inspired by the sight of an ancient Norman church, a church which still stands in Usk today. As he views this church Eliot realises that these ancient legends are of much less significance than mankind's ability to build objects that will outlast him. The church he was looking at was almost 800 years old and its builders were long since dead and gone. This strikes Eliot as something magical and extraordinary, and he realises that there is no need to seek out the extraordinary in fantasy, when so much of it occurs in daily reality. This is the environment surrounding us communicating in a truly meaningful and inspirational way.

In these four poems I have attempted to explain how these poets were inspired to write by different landscapes, and how the way that they were inspired is not all that different from the way the environment communicates with each and every one of us. It is important to realise that poets and poets' minds function in much the same way as those of other people and that poetry is much more accessible, and indeed enjoyable, than most people realise at first.

Exercises

1. Take a piece of poetry of your own choosing (if you cannot think of any, ask your teacher to select one for you), and write a short piece about how you feel the environment in the poem was communicating with the poet as they wrote it.

2. Select a physical landscape that you enjoy spending time in and write a short piece about how you feel it communicates with you, i.e. how it makes you feel while you're there and why.

Note: *any physical environment can be used for this; it does not necessarily have to be outdoors, or be a place that others would consider beautiful. The piece does not have to be a poem, but may be so if you wish.*

Summary

We are constantly receiving messages from the physical environment that surrounds us, through shape, colour, texture, smell and through sound. Our state of mind can affect the feelings our environment evokes; for example, if we are in a negative mood we are more likely to receive a negative message from our surroundings. Our own obsessions and concerns can affect what we see and how we see it. Our surroundings can frequently trigger memories within us, most often through a sound or smell. On top of this, our environment can also offer deep insights. On occasion the beauty of the natural world can fill us with joy and inspiration.

The physical environment does not always have a positive effect on us. It can also depress us and fill us with stress. Yet, when stressed, people often use a mental sanctuary to allow them to relax and calm their minds. They remember a time when they felt more at home in their surroundings. For some people, their contact with their environment is how they experience spirituality in their lives.

The history of a region can also alter how we perceive an environment, and change the feelings it inspires in us. This history can be actual or legendary. Frequently, history adds a great deal of meaning to a physical mindscape.

The best way of ensuring that we respond positively to our environment is by engaging with our environment in a positive and rewarding way.

Learners will be able to:

- describe the various uses of technology to assist communication
- use a range of communication technologies to exchange information with another user
- explain the impact of communication and information technology on personal, social and vocational life
- outline current relevant legislation in terms of rights, responsibilities, grievances and penalties.

Unit 4

Communication Technology

SECTION 1
Communication Technology

Learning Outcomes

Learners will:

- be able to describe the different types of communication technology tools and their main features.

Introduction

Nowadays there are many tools available to assist communication. Using data from the Central Statistics Office (CSO) and other surveys, the most popular tools will be identified and evaluated in this section. It will also explore the impact of these tools on our lives today. Students are expected to demonstrate the uses of ICT tools as part of the assessment criteria for the FETAC Level 5 communications module. This book will provide detailed instructions on sending and receiving emails, texting and surfing the internet.

Modern communication trends

A survey was published recently by a company in Boston (Prompt Communications), which specialises in public relations, marketing and social networking. The survey shows that social networking tools are becoming popular, but more traditional methods of communication are still widely used. The following are the main results of the survey.

- The telephone is still the most popular method of communication. Of 300 respondents, 99 per cent said that they use the telephone regularly.
- Facebook, a social networking tool, came in as the second most popular method of communication (96 per cent).
- Short messaging service (SMS), or text messaging, is the next most popular method at 93 per cent.
- Email was used by 91 per cent of respondents.
- The communication method used most frequently is SMS, followed by Facebook and then the telephone.

ICT trends closer to home will be examined later. First, we will look at the various information technology tools that assist communication.

The telephone

The telephone is still the most popular method of communication. Telephones enable people to talk to each other over long distances and are widely used in homes, businesses and organisations. Landline telephones are connected using a phone line. Providers in Ireland include Eircom, Gaelic Telecom, BT, etc. Other companies use a satellite connection, for example UPC. Landline telephone manufacturers have developed handsets that operate a limited 'wireless' capability; these allow the user to walk around the house while on the phone.

Mobile telephone

Mobile telephones or cell phones have become increasingly popular since their invention in 1973 by Martin Cooper, who worked in Motorola. Mobile phones have developed from simple devices, which enabled people to talk or send SMS texts, to devices that allow the users to send pictures, surf the net, send emails, listen

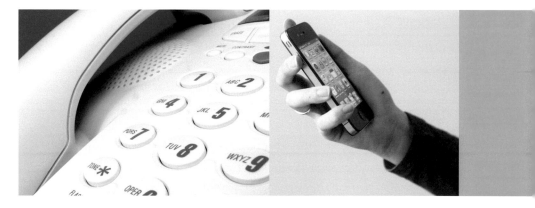

to music, etc. In fact, mobile phones now have so many functions it is getting more difficult to distinguish them from smartphones. Some mobile phones allow the user to send both SMS and multimedia messaging service (MMS) texts.

Texting

Many feel that texting language is detrimental to the English language. However, texting is a very popular method of communication, and it is useful to know some of the texting abbreviations that have evolved as a result. The following is a list of the most common abbreviations.

Abbreviation	Meaning
2moro	tomorrow
2nite	tonight
B4N	bye for now
BCNU	be seeing you
BFF	best friends forever
BRB	be right back
BTW	by the way
CYA	see you
FWIW	for what it's worth
GR8	great
ILY	I love you

IMHO	in my humble opinion
IRL	in real life
ISO	in search of
JK	just kidding
L8R	later
LOL	laugh out loud
	lots of love
NP	no problem
	nosy parents
OIC	oh, I see
OMG	oh my god
POV	point of view
RBTL	read between the lines
RT	real time
RTM	read the manual
THX or TX or THKS	thanks
TLC	tender loving care
TMI	too much information
TTYL	talk to you later
TYVM	thank you very much

Source: http://www.netlingo.com/top50/popular-text-terms.php

Smartphone

There are many types of smartphone on the market today. As already mentioned, mobile phones have many of the functions that smartphones offer, so it is getting increasingly difficult to distinguish between the two. The BlackBerry smartphone illustrated opposite (www.blackberry.com), is just one example of the many types of smartphone on the market today. Smartphones have a number of features but usually include voice-activated dialling, conference calling, SMS and MMS text messaging, sharing pictures, videos and files, sending and receiving emails, viewing attachments to emails, sending voice notes as email attachments.

Smartphones go a step further by syncing with the email server of your personal or corporate provider. Smartphones also allow users to access instant messaging and social networking applications. Some smartphones are equipped with GPS (global positioning system) software. Android and Symbian smartphones are currently competing well with Apple's iPhone.

Personal digital assistant

A personal digital assistant (PDA) is also known as a palmtop computer. This is because it is small enough to fit in the palm of your hand. This device is a personal organiser used to manage contacts, appointments and to-do lists. PDAs also connect to the internet. This device comes equipped with a touch screen facility and often the keyboard is part of the touch screen. PDA functions have now been combined with mobile phones and media players.

The computer

The computer is a key information and communications technology (ICT) tool in business and society in general. The type of computer needed depends on the functions required by the user. If you are using standard applications for email, word processing, spreadsheets and accounts, you would not need an expensive, top of the range computer.

Some functions of computers
- Producing documents such as letters.
- Performing calculations in spreadsheets, for example budgets.

- Delivering presentations with applications such as Microsoft PowerPoint.
- Entering data into databases.
- Surfing the internet.
- Sending and receiving emails.

Desktop computer

As the name suggests, this computer is meant for a workstation such as an office desk. This type of computer needs to be plugged into a power socket and therefore it is not easily moved around. Desktop computers are widely used in homes and offices.

Some features to look out for when purchasing a desktop computer:
- The speed of the central processing unit (CPU). This is the brain of the computer. The speed of the CPU is measured in GHz (gigahertz) and current speeds are in or around 2.5GHz.
- The amount of random access memory (RAM). The more RAM the computer has, the faster it will be. Desktops nowadays have around 4GB of RAM. Memory is measured in bytes and one gigabyte contains one billion bytes.
- The amount of space on the hard disk you require. Hard disks now have memory capacity of up to 1TB (terabyte). This means the computer hard disk can store approximately one trillion bytes. The amount of hard disk space required depends on what you need it for. Graphics, photos, movies and audio files take up more space than files such as documents and spreadsheets.
- The operating system is also important as this runs all the other applications on the computer. Windows is the operating system we are most familiar with. Different versions are available depending on the user's needs.

Laptop

A laptop is a portable computer. The laptop has all of the required elements in one unit, i.e. the motherboard, CPU, hard drive, visual display unit (VDU), etc. One could argue that a laptop is essentially a portable desktop. However, laptops do not have as much processing power or hard drive capacity as a desktop computer. CPU speeds are around 2.5 GHz, RAM 4GB and hard disk capacity 500GB.

Notebook

Notebooks are for users who would like reasonably good processing power, with more portability. Notebooks essentially provide a lot of the same functions as laptops, with a few differences. There is no internal DVD or CD drive, and notebooks have a small keyboard and a minimal graphics system. Notebooks are smaller and lighter than laptops.

Tablet PC

A tablet PC is a mobile computer shaped like a thin, rectangular slab. Tablet PCs have a touchscreen and a stylus pen is used to input data. Some tablet PCs are convertible (they come with an attachable keyboard) and can be used both as a notebook and as a tablet PC.

Multimedia players

These devices store pictures, videos and songs and are more commonly known as MP3 players. The type of MP3 device you buy will depend on how much storage you want and whether you want it for playing music, videos or both. The Apple iPod is the most popular type of MP3 player. Other makers are SanDisk and Zone. Users can listen to music on these devices via earphones and some can be placed in a 'docking' device which contains speakers.

Further developments

Technology is continually developing. As previously mentioned, companies are always coming up with new devices for communication. Mobile phones nowadays can have all the functions of a smartphone, PDA and an MP3 player. The iPhone, developed by Apple, was designed to combine the mobile phone with the iPod.

Apple launched the new iPad in April 2010. This is a tablet device. Its main functions are email, photos, watching videos, downloading music and books (from iTunes and iBooks respectively), mapping, keeping notes, personal organiser and storing contacts. It also contains software for word processing and spreadsheets. When docked it can be used as a digital photoframe or alarm clock. The only thing that the iPad currently can't do is make voice phone calls. It is also widely hoped that the iPad will be equipped with a camera for video conferencing (http://www.apple.com/ipad/features/).

The internet

The majority of the devices discussed here are equipped with software for browsing the internet. Let us look in more detail at the internet and the communication tools it has to offer.

The internet is a global network of interconnected networks. A computer can communicate with any other computer as long as they are both connected to the internet. The internet allows users to search for and find information on a wide variety of topics using search engines and it is also possible to publish information on the internet.

The internet is not the world wide web (www). The world wide web is part of the internet. The world wide web can be viewed as a worldwide library containing information sourced from web pages. These web pages are stored in different computers all over the world. The internet is what connects everything together. A website is a collection of web pages. Companies and organisations are using websites more and more as communication tools to provide information about their products and services. Websites can be used to provide information using a variety of methods of communication.

To connect to the internet you will need software, such as Internet Explorer, Safari, Google Chrome or Mozilla Firefox. An internet service provider (ISP) is also needed. ISPs in Ireland include Eircom, 3, Vodafone, Permanet, Meteor, etc. A modem, telephone line or satellite connection, as well as a computer, are needed to get connected.

Search engines

Search engines such as Google, Yahoo, AltaVista, MSN and Bing allow users to gather information about a variety of topics. Search engines can also be used to find out about new products or services and to compare prices and other items from different companies.

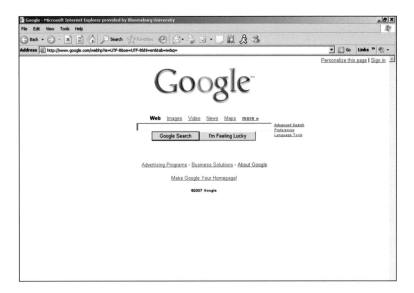

Using a search engine

- First, type in the address of the search engine in the address bar of the internet browser (e.g. Internet Explorer, Safari, Google Chrome or Mozilla Firefox). For example: www.google.com
- In the search box provided, type in the search terms.
  Tips
  - The search can be made more specific by using the + symbol, for example Music + Razorlight, will display information relating to music by the band Razorlight.
  - For a more specific search use the Advanced Search option.
  - Putting a sentence in inverted commas will look for that exact phrase.
- Press enter.
- A list of web pages will be displayed. Each web page will have a link, usually in blue. Underneath the link will be an extract of text from the web page. This text should give the user an idea whether or not the web page will

provide the information required. If the site is unsuitable, press the back button. The back button is usually located on the top left of the internet browser. It is easy to identify the sites that have been visited already as they will now be in purple. Once a link has been clicked on it changes to purple.

Exercise

Downloading information from the internet.

(This exercise can be used to meet the assessment criteria for Communication Technology Skills.)

Using a search engine, students are asked to provide three different quotations for a holiday to Marbella. Prices should include flights, accommodation and car hire.

Email

Email is similar to 'snail' mail except that letters are delivered electronically over the internet instead of using the postman.

Advantages of email	Disadvantages
Fast, efficient	Security – emails can be intercepted, though encryption is being used to stamp out this threat
Emails are free	Reading attached files can be difficult if you don't have the correct software
Other files can be attached to an email and multiple copies can be sent	Computer viruses can be spread via email
Environmentally friendly	It is easy to send an email to the wrong person

Using email

There are many different email providers. Setting up an email account is easy. On almost any email provider's website you will find a link with words similar to 'sign up now'. Clicking on this link will navigate the user to another page. You will be asked to input your name and some other details. You will need to choose an email address, and this address will be unique to you. A password also needs to be input. You will use your email address and password to sign in to your email account. No matter which email provider you use the method of sending an email is essentially the same. To begin writing an email click on 'New' or 'Compose'.

Writing an email

Layout of an email

To: name@emailprovider.com

CC: name2@emailprovider.com, name3@emailprovider.com

BCC: name4@emailprovider.com

Subject   How to write an email

Body of an email

Dear Students

Here is information on how to write an email.

The 'To' field should contain the email address of the person you are writing to. The format of this address will be the person's user name, the '@' symbol, followed by the name of the email provider (examples include Yahoo, Google, Hotmail, Eircom). The last part of the email address refers to the country or whether or not the email provider is a company or network. Here are some examples:

name@eircom.net

name@google.com

name@hotmail.com

name@yahoo.ie

The 'CC' field stands for carbon copy. At the end of a letter or memo there might be the letters 'CC' with the names of people next to it. This means that a copy of the letter or memo has been sent to these people. It is the same for an email. The 'CC' field is used to input the email addresses of people who should get a copy of the email.

The 'BCC' field is also used for this purpose but BCC stands for Blind Carbon Copy. This means that the recipients in the 'To' and 'CC' fields will not see the email addresses contained in this field.

Emails can be sent to multiple recipients by adding a comma between addresses.

The 'Subject' field should contain an indication of what the email is about.

Finally, the last section is the body of the email.

Once the email has been written, proofread and spell checked, click 'Send'.

Attaching a file to an email

A file can be attached to an email by clicking on the paper clip icon while creating the email. The user can then browse for the file they wish to attach and click 'Attach'. If the file is large it will take a while to attach to the email.

Opening emails

An email you receive will be displayed in the 'Inbox' with a link to open it. The inbox will show who sent the email and also the subject of the email. To open the email click on the link.

Downloading an attachment

The paper clip symbol tells the receiver that there is a file attached. When the email has an attachment, the paper clip will be displayed next to it, in the receiver's inbox. Open the email as normal. At the end of the body of the text or at the top of the email near the subject, the attachment file will be displayed.

Depending on the email application being used, you may have the option to view the file as HTML. This means that the file will be displayed in a web browser such as Internet Explorer. The other option is to download the file. To do this, either click on the file itself, or click the word 'Download', displayed as a link next to the file name or in a separate window after the file name has been clicked. The download option will not be available until the file has been scanned for viruses. Once download has been clicked, the computer will display a message saying 'Do you want to open or save this file?' Saving the file will download it to the computer hard drive, and the user can view the file later. If the user chooses 'Open', the file will be displayed after it has been downloaded.

The length of time it takes to download an attachment will depend on how large the file is. Videos, songs and pictures will take longer to download than documents or spreadsheets. Sometimes larger files can be compressed into a zip folder, which reduces the size of the files, until they are extracted by the user. The compressed folder looks like a folder with a zip on it. Once the contents have been extracted, the normal folder icon will be displayed.

Replying to an email

To reply to an email, click on the 'Reply' button. Where this button is displayed will depend on the email provider you are using. The reply button will be displayed using the text 'Reply' or an icon. (Placing the mouse cursor over the icon should display text telling the user the function of the button.) Once 'Reply' has been selected, a window similar to the window for composing an email will be displayed. The 'To' field will already have the email address of the person being replied to. The subject field will also be filled in with the letters 'Re:' before it. The receiver has now become the sender of the email, and the 'CC' and 'BCC' options are still available.

As with composing an email from scratch, the message will be typed in the main section of the email. The original message will also be displayed, but this can be deleted if the user so wishes. Now all there is left to do is proofread and spell check the email and click on 'Send'.

Forwarding an email

If the receiver of an email feels that the information it contains would be useful to another person, email applications offer a forwarding function. Again this function will be displayed using the text 'Forward' or an icon. Once clicked, a window will be displayed. This time the user must fill in the email addresses of the recipients in the 'To' field, and again the 'CC' and 'BCC' options are available. The subject field will be filled in with the letters 'Fwd:' before it. The original message will be displayed in the main section of the email, and the sender has an option to include some text of their own before the main message to explain the source of the email, for example, 'Here is something I thought you would find interesting. Kind Regards, Michael.' Once all the details have been input, proofread and spell check the message and click on 'Send'.

Netiquette

Netiquette comes from the word etiquette, which means good manners. Netiquette simply refers to good manners on the internet. Remember, email is a form of communication and common courtesy still applies. Here are some useful points:

- As with any other print media, the sender should not include language that the receiver will not understand. If the receiver cannot understand the message, clarification will have to be sought and this can waste time.
- It is widely perceived that an email written in capital letters is the same as shouting. Sentence case should be used, that is, use a capital letter at the beginning of a sentence only.
- Avoid putting critical comments in an email. This is known as 'flaming'. Email is not an appropriate medium of communication for negative or critical comments. Any problems should be resolved in person where possible, or else over the phone. People often say that they would put things in an email that they would never say face to face. The same goes for text messages on mobile phones. Things like 'You're fired' should never be put in an email. If you are unable to say it in person, don't put it in an email.
- Emails at work should be used to communicate factual information only. The company email should not be used for sending jokes, funny pictures, etc. Managers have been criticised for giving instructions about a job in an email. This can lead to all sorts of difficulties if the receiver misunderstands the message.
- The sender should not forward 'spam', more commonly known as junk mail, to the receiver. Email users find this type of mail very annoying, and often delete the email without reading it. Of course, spam can also contain harmful

viruses, so it is generally advised that an email should not be opened unless you know the sender.

- Avoid sending attachments that will take the receiver a long time to download. For sending large files, mail servers such as sendspace (www.sendspace.com) or transferbigfiles (www.transferbigfiles.com) can be used. However, a lot of email providers offer email users a large amount of memory which means the user may never have to delete another email. Also, broadband speeds are improving all the time and this will significantly reduce the amount of time it takes to download an attachment.

- The sender should be careful about the information contained in an email. There is always a chance that an email could be intercepted by a third party. Email providers use encryption to stop this. Encryption makes an email unreadable if a third party intercepts it. The email will be in the format of unreadable code until it reaches the receiver. In general, avoid putting confidential information in an email and remember company emails are not private, as copies of these emails can be stored for years. Companies such as banks continually warn their customers that the institution will never email them asking for their account details, so don't fall prey to such requests from other sources.

- Always proofread the email before sending it. Internet slang such as LOL (laugh out loud), FYI (for your information), OMG (oh my god) should be avoided in any formal communication. When using internet slang in informal communication make sure that the receiver understands the terminology.

- Emotion icons can be added to an email to communicate feelings. For example, :-) means the person is happy, :-(means the person is sad, ;-) is a wink. Internet slang dictionaries and translators are available on the internet (Conlin, 2002; Nielsen Business Media, 1998).

Exercise

Summarise the information that you gathered from the exercise 'Downloading information from the internet'.

Type this summary using a word processing application, and save it with the file name 'Holiday'. Using an email application, send an

---

email to one of your classmates using the following as the subject and body of the message:

Subject: Holiday to Marbella

Message:

Dear _____

Attached is a document detailing three different quotations for a holiday to Marbella. The quotations include flights, accommodation and car rental.

Kind regards

(Your name)

Using the CC field, send a copy of the email to another classmate, or the class tutor. Attach the holiday document to the email. Spell check and proofread the email and send it.

Contacts

Email applications provide the user with a facility for storing contact information. The applications will differ but the following table shows the contact information that can be stored.

Contact details

Name	Company name	Email address
Address	Company address	Website
Home phone number	Work email	Birthday
Mobile phone number	Work phone	

Managing email accounts

- Delete unwanted emails from the Inbox to free up the account.
- Delete unwanted mail from the Sent folder. This folder keeps a copy of all the emails that have been sent. Be sure to keep a record of important emails, such as job applications.
- Folders can be created to organise messages that you wish to keep. Icons such as flags or stars can be placed next to important emails. An email can also be marked as 'unread' to remind the user that even though the email was opened, it was not read.
- Empty the Trash folder regularly. Some email providers do this automatically.

Voice over Internet Protocol

This is a communication technology that allows users to make telephone calls over the internet. To use this type of technology, the user must have broadband.

Voice over Internet Protocol (VoIP) can be used by the following methods:

1. Connecting a standard telephone to the computer or internet connection using a device called an analogue telephone adaptor (ATA).
2. By using an IP phone, which is a special phone that connects directly to the router or broadband modem.
3. Communicating via computer to computer. For this method, both users will need a microphone, speakers (internal or external), a soundcard, and be connected to the internet via broadband. If both computers have a webcam installed, the users will also be able to see each other. (O'Neill and Morgan, 2007).

Skype is the most popular internet telephony company in Ireland. The software needed can be downloaded free from Skype's website. It has the following features:

1. free calls to anyone on Skype
2. free video calls
3. subscription or pay as you go options for calling landlines and mobile phones, and SMS text messaging
4. voicemail and call forwarding to your own mobile or home phone if you miss a call.

Skype can be downloaded from www.skype.com.

Instant messaging

Instant messaging is communicating in real time over the internet using an instant messaging program. The message is sent from one computer and is displayed immediately on the receiver's computer. Instant messaging programs also allow the user to store a list of contacts with whom they chat regularly. Once the internet is launched, the program will automatically generate a list of friends online who are ready to chat. Here are some of the features of the most popular instant messaging programs.

- Send instant messages to one friend or hold a conference with a number of friends.
- Get updates on what friends are up to from social networking sites such as Twitter, Facebook and Flickr.
- Check email, news and weather.
- Make PC-to-PC calls or PC-to-phone calls; PC-to-PC calls are free and require the user to have a microphone and speakers or headphones.
- Video calling.
- Send text messages to friends' mobiles for free. However, they will get charged for the text!
- Watch web videos and view photos with friends, play games.
- Use messenger on mobile phone.

Examples of instant messaging services include:
- Yahoo! Messenger – http://messenger.yahoo.com/
- Windows Live Messenger – http://windowslive.com/desktop/messenger
- Google Talk – http://www.google.com/talk/
- AIM – www.aim.com

Internet relay chat

Internet relay chat (IRC) allows people to communicate with each other on IRC networks around the world in real time. Users can hold group conferences or one-to-one private discussions. An IRC channel is a chat room where users discuss a common interest. To join an IRC channel, an IRC application must be stored on the user's computer. mIRC is a popular Windows IRC program.

Summary

There are many options available to us nowadays to communicate socially or for business. Technology has made it possible for us to communicate with people all over the world via telephone, video conferencing, internet and email, etc. It is important that the right communication tool is chosen to get the message across. For important messages that require instant feedback and clarification, two-way conversation methods such as the telephone or video conferencing might be appropriate. Instant messaging, internet chat and, to a certain extent, SMS text messaging may be more appropriate for communicating with friends or family. In conclusion, information technology has given us communication tools for most situations. How we choose to use them is up to us.

Exercises

1. Explain the differences between a mobile phone and a smart-phone.

2. What are the main factors to consider when buying a computer?

3. Distinguish between a laptop and a notebook.

4. Identify ten common text message abbreviations.

5. Why do people use search engines on the internet?

6. What is email?

7. List the main elements that should be included when sending an email.

8. Briefly list four netiquette rules.

9. Send an email to two of your classmates using the 'To' and 'CC' fields. The subject of the email is 'class party'. The body of the email should include details of the class party venue, date and time.

10. What is VoIP?

11. List four features of instant messaging programmes.

12. What is the most popular internet telephony company in Ireland?

The Age of Social Networking

Learning Outcomes

Learners will:
- understand the purpose of social networking
- recognise the features of the most common social networking websites.

Introduction

Social networking websites offer a new way of staying in touch with family and friends. Whether or not you are a fan of social networking, these types of site are changing the way individuals, businesses and organisations communicate. This section will explore some of the more popular social networking websites and look at their main features.

Facebook

Facebook is a social networking website that allows the user to stay in touch with friends and family all over the world.

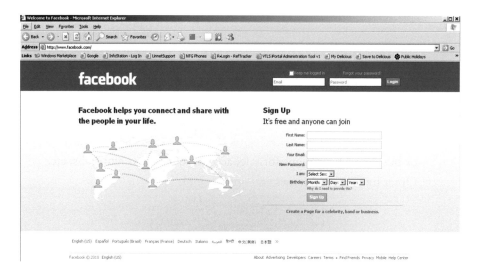

http://www.facebook.com/

Features:

- When signing up to Facebook, you will have the option to make your page public or private. It is recommended that everybody should keep their page private, unless it is for business. This way the user has control over who can see their profile; they have the option to either accept or deny friend requests.

- You can find friends using the friend search box, either by name, the school they went to, location, or by using an email account. If their page is private you will have to send them a friend request. It is only when they accept your request that you can view their profile and vice versa.

- When the user logs on to Facebook, his or her home page will be displayed. The home page displays a newsfeed, which allows the user to keep up to date with what his or her friends have been doing. The following are the main contents of the home page:
  - Newsfeed – this feature allows the user to control which friends they want to see updates from, and what applications they want to use. Facebook has a lot of applications (a lot of games) and the activity of friends on these applications is displayed in the Newsfeed section. This can clutter the user's homepage, so it is worth taking the time to customise the page.
  - Messages – send private messages to friends, view inbox and outbox, almost like using an email application. The message facility allows the

user to send attachments, but there is no 'CC' feature for sending copies of the message to other friends.

- Events – this section allows the user to let friends and family know about upcoming events.
- Photos – this is a link that displays all the recent photos and videos uploaded by friends.
- Marketplace – this provides a link to an advertisement page where people or businesses have items for sale, accommodation to rent, jobs, etc.
- Other links are for games and applications.

- Profile page
  - Wall – this page displays the user's wall, where the user can write status updates (what they have been up to) and where friends can also write comments.
  - Info – this section of the page is where the user puts some information about themselves, for example hobbies, favourite films, books.
  - Photos – users can upload photos to share with friends and family. Photos can be organised by album.
  - Notes – this is a blogging feature; a blog is like an online diary.
  - Links – post useful links for your friends.

- Other features
  - Facebook will notify you when a friend's birthday is coming up.
  - Users can join group pages, or become a fan of pages created by others.
  - You can keep in touch with Facebook using a Facebook application on your mobile phone.
  - Friends can chat privately using Facebook Chat.
  - Privacy options allow the user to control which friends can see status updates and photos, etc.

MySpace

MySpace is also a popular social networking site, although many commentators remark that Facebook is currently the most popular. Many music industry professionals and radio DJs have MySpace pages. MySpace is a very popular social networking site for bands; they use it for posting their latest songs, videos and upcoming concerts.

Features

- Find friends.
- Stay in touch with family.
- Map your family tree.
- Mail Center: for sending and receiving mail and managing friend requests.
- View updates from friends.
- There is an events section where you can notify people about an upcoming event and invite them to attend.
- Instant messaging.
- Share photos and videos.
- Access content on mobile phones.
- Get Really Simple Syndication (RSS) feeds with the latest new stories.
- Listen to your favourite music, watch your favourite television shows.
- Classified ads.
- Polls.
- Blog – users can post blogs themselves or view the blogs created by other people.
- As with Facebook, MySpace gives the user control over who can view their profile.

Twitter

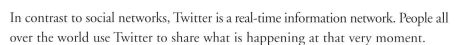

In contrast to social networks, Twitter is a real-time information network. People all over the world use Twitter to share what is happening at that very moment.

Features

- When a person signs up for Twitter, he or she can choose the topics that they are interested in, for example music, or a certain band.
- He/she can also find friends on Twitter, or other people such as movie stars, and choose to 'follow' them. When you follow a person, each time they tweet (i.e. write something), you will see it on your home page.
- The first section of Twitter is the user's homepage, which shows posts that you have entered ('tweets'), and allows you to read tweets from friends, celebrities, bands, companies, radio DJs, etc.
- The profile section shows your own tweets.
- Twitter has a goodies section. For example, Widgets allow the user to

display their Twitter updates on their webpage or other social networking pages such as Facebook or MySpace.

- You can send a private message to somebody that you are following.
- As opposed to Facebook or MySpace, pictures cannot be added using the Twitter application, but a third-party application can be used to post pictures or videos.
- Privacy options allow you to make your page private. Twitter automatically sets up your page as public. This means that your 'tweets' will appear on a search, so if a user is looking for information on a particular topic, and you have written about it, it will show up.
- Twitter has a set of rules that should be followed and these can be checked on the following link: http://twitter.zendesk.com/forums/26257/entries/18311

Flickr

Flickr (https://www.flickr.com/tour) is a website for sharing and managing photos and videos.

Features

- Users can upload photographs and videos from their computer or camera phone or send them to Flickr by email.
- Photos can be edited, for example for red eye, cropping, font and effects.
- Photos and videos can be organised by collections.
- Users can share photos with friends and family. Privacy controls allow the user to control who can see the photos, add notes or comments. Notes will only appear when the user moves the mouse over the picture, whereas comments appear separately underneath the picture.
- Maps – this is a very useful application on Flickr. Users can map photos or videos by dragging and dropping them with the mouse onto where they were taken on the world map. Users can also browse the world map to view photos and videos taken by other people in different locations.
- Using 'Snapfish', users can use their photos to make prints, cards, photo books, calendars or canvas.
- Relatives and friends who are not on Flickr can be given a guest pass, which allows them to view your photos.

Summary

Social networking sites provide a new way of communicating. They are especially useful for staying in touch with family and friends abroad.

Exercise

1. What is the function of social networking websites?

2. By looking at Facebook and MySpace, compile a list of common features.

3. Distinguish between Twitter and the other social networking websites.

4. What is Flickr?

5. In your opinion, is social networking a good method of communication?

6. Do you think that tools such as Facebook and Twitter could be integrated into the classroom?

The Impact of ICT

Introduction

Information and communications technology (ICT) has proved to be a powerful tool in increasing productivity, creating jobs, generating economic growth, removing communication barriers and, with the aid of e-business, removing trade barriers. Businesses can enter global markets more easily. Marketing and advertising products and services has also become simpler. Friends and family can now stay in touch with the aid of ICT tools such as Skype and social networking websites.

Unfortunately, the internet has a downside. It has become a platform for terrorists to communicate and plan attacks. Children may become exposed to cyber bullying, inappropriate content and online predators via chat rooms and social networking sites. So what is the overall impact of ICT on society and business? This section will look at how ICT is used in business and in the home, and the extent of its use. We will then look at how social networking websites are revolutionising business. Finally, we will look at some causes for concern and what can be done to eliminate the risks associated with communicating over the internet.

Use of ICT in business

The Central Statistics Office (CSO) published 'Information Society Statistics for 2010'. Here are some of the main points:

- 92 per cent of all enterprises had a computer connected to the internet
- 68 per cent of all enterprises had a website or homepage.

The internet is used in enterprises:

- to communicate to customers about their products and price lists via online catalogues
- for banking and financial services
- to interact with public authorities, for example filling out forms
- for training and information, for example training employees.

E-commerce

E-commerce involves buying and selling goods or services over the internet. The

2010 CSO survey shows that:
- 44 per cent of enterprises use e-commerce for purchases
- 21 per cent of enterprises use e-commerce for sales
- 21 per cent of all purchases were over the internet
- 44 per cent of all sales were over the internet.

The most recent survey available on the use of ICT, the CSO's Information Society and Telecommunications Survey (2008), found that one-quarter of all enterprises believe that ICT has made a significant improvement in the reorganisation and simplification of work routines. When asked about barriers to e-commerce, some enterprises felt that a number of products are not suitable for sale on the internet and that customers may not be ready to use internet commerce. Others had concerns about the security of doing business over the internet and there was also some uncertainty concerning the legal framework.

Social networking – revolutionising business

Businesses now use internet tools to connect with their customers. Their websites communicate information about products and services. E-commerce allows them to buy and sell goods over the internet. And businesses are using social networking as a communication medium for customer relationship management. Most musicians, for example, are using MySpace to promote their songs and concerts; similarly, businesses have started using Facebook to connect with their customers, and more and more businesses are using Twitter as a customer relationship tool.

Unlike Facebook, or other social networking websites, Twitter has a search facility: 'Find out what people are saying about..'. Businesses are starting to utilise this search facility to find out what people are saying about their company, products and/or services. Twitter has become the preferred medium of communication for more than 50 million executives, celebrities, athletes and ordinary people. Before joining Twitter, a business can first study what their customers are saying and what they want. Twitter is a method of conversation, a facility and it is almost like an ongoing customer satisfaction survey, as it communicates in real time what people like or dislike about the product or service. The business can then decide to enter the Twitter conversation and reach out to their customers.

Social networking websites and Twitter can be used to talk about new products, new services and promotions that the company is planning. If the business updates information regularly they will manage to keep their customers' interest. Twitter has various different applications for business such as 'TwtQpon' for creating coupons, or 'monitter', which is a live streaming view. Monitter can be used on Twitter to see what people are saying about the company (Ankeny, 2009).

The internet can be used as a cheap method of communication for companies to advertise and market their products and services. But remember not everybody is on the internet and not everybody uses social networking websites, so the company will need to know their customer base before deciding whether or not the internet is a suitable communication tool for them.

Use of ICT in the home

In its 2008 study the CSO also found that:

- one million households had a computer at home
- 92 per cent of persons aged 16–42 have used a computer, compared with 31 per cent of those aged 65–74
- 87 per cent of those aged 16–24 have used the internet, whereas in the age group 66–74 the figure is 22 per cent
- computer and internet usage is highest among students, followed by those at work.

Hierarchy of internet activity

The most popular activities are information search and online services, which are broken down into the following:

- travel and accommodation
- downloading software
- reading/downloading newspapers or magazines
- job hunting, and applying for jobs online
- finding health-related information.

The survey also showed that more and more people are buying goods over the internet; 1.2 million people ordered goods or services over the internet for their own use.

Telecommunications

The Information Society and Telecommunications Survey (2008) contains figures from the Commission for Communications Regulation (ComReg) in Ireland. Here are some interesting statistics:

- 20.3 billion minutes of voice calls (including calls from mobiles) were made in 2008.
- 10.1 billion SMS messages were sent.
- the number of subscribers to satellite or cable TV has increased.

A more recent survey, published by ComReg on 24 March 2010, shows that the average time spent on the internet per week has increased from ten hours in December 2008 to over thirteen hours in January 2010.

Some concerns

Webwise carried out a survey in 2006 regarding children's use of the internet. Here are some of main findings from that survey (the children questioned were in the 9–16 age group).

- 50 per cent of teenagers and 25 per cent of preteens chat on the internet.
- 27 per cent of the children questioned said they had met someone new on the internet who asked for private information, for example their photo, phone number, home address or school address.
- 19 per cent of children who use chat facilities such as instant messaging said they had been harassed, upset, bothered, threatened or embarrassed by a person they were chatting to.
- 7 per cent of children had arranged to meet personally someone they had met on the internet. Of these, 24 per cent said that the person they had met had turned out to be an adult, having introduced themselves as a child on the internet.
- Over 50 per cent of children stated that their parents don't speak, or rarely speak to them about their activity on the internet.
- Worryingly, there has been an increase in the number of children willing to give out personal information over the internet, compared to the last survey in 2003. In Ireland, 27 per cent of the children questioned were prepared to disclose their full name and email address.

Summary

Many businesses feel that ICT has generally improved business operations. Mundane tasks that would otherwise take hours can be completed in minutes. Businesses can reach their customers in more ways than ever before. Individuals can order goods and services, and search for information from the comfort of their own home. Friends and family can stay in touch all over the world.

However, the internet, in particular, does have some drawbacks. The more information there is out there about you, the greater the possibility that the information will get into the wrong hands. Children are particularly vulnerable when it comes to giving out information to the wrong people.

In conclusion, it should be remembered that communication technology tools are designed to enhance how we communicate, not to replace the more traditional method of communication, which is face to face. There is a danger that we will become so caught up in the age of technology that we will forget how to use the more traditional methods of communication. It is up to us to make sure that this does not happen.

Exercises

1. How is the internet used by business?

2. List two reasons why a business would not use the internet to sell their goods or services.

3. Do you use a social networking website? If so, how cautious are you when it comes to allowing new people to view your profile? What is the main risk involved in increasing your number of friends?

4. How can businesses use social networking websites to connect with their customers?

5. What rules would you put in place in your household to ensure the safety of children while they are surfing the internet?

SECTION 4
Legislation

Learning Outcomes

Learners will:
- know the rights of individuals under the Data Protection Acts
- understand the responsibilities of data controllers or protectors
- understand the Freedom of Information Act, and what information is exempt under this Act.

Introduction

As it is becoming increasingly easier to access information using ICT tools, legislation has been put in place to govern how this information is used.

Data Protection Acts 1988 and 2003

Data protection involves keeping personal information given to companies private and safe. Individuals have the right to data protection when their details are held on a computer, in hard copy files, audio or visual clips. Data protection ensures that the information kept about an individual must be factually correct, only available to the correct bodies and used for the stated purposes only.

Rights of individuals

- Personal details should be used in line with the legislation.
- Individuals have the right to know if an organisation or individual is holding their details, the identity of that organisation or individual and what they want the details for.
- An individual has the right to access any information that is being kept about him or her.
- A person can enquire from an organisation if they are holding their personal details and, if it is, the organisation must disclose this.
- An individual has the right to remove or edit information being held about them by an individual or an organisation. They also have the right to stop an organisation using personal details for anything other than what the information was collected for.
- An individual can have his or her details removed from direct marketing lists, and to refuse direct marketing calls or mail. To do this an individual can get their phone number entered on the National Directory Database. It is an offence to contact anybody on this database.

Responsibilities of data controllers

- A data controller is an organisation or specified person that holds information about an individual.
- The information must be obtained and processed fairly.
- The information kept must be serving one or more purposes and these purposes must be lawful. The information must be kept only for the length of time it takes to serve this purpose and it should be relevant and sufficient for that purpose.
- Once the purpose or purposes have been specified, information can only be processed for that purpose.
- The information must be kept safe and secure.
- The information must be kept accurate and up to date.
- If an individual requests his or her personal information the data controller must give a copy of the information being held.
  (http://www.dataprotection.ie/)

Freedom of Information Act 1998 and 2003

This Act allows individuals access to information held by government departments and some public bodies. One is entitled to get information about oneself free of charge; any other requests must be accompanied by a fee.

The following are exempt from the Act:

- government meetings
- law enforcement and security
- confidential and commercially sensitive information
- personal information (when not being requested by the person to whom the information relates).

In other countries, similar Acts have been shown to improve the decisions that are made by public servants. This is because public servants know the information can be seen by the public. The Act also attempts to stamp out a 'cover up' culture. Much information that is in the public interest has come to light over the last number of years because of media requesting information under the Freedom of Information Act. (http://www.foi.gov.ie/)

Summary

The Data Protection Acts' main function is to govern how personal information is being used. The Acts are there to protect us as individuals. The Freedom of Information Act has created a more open and accountable society. It is important as an individual that you familiarise yourself with your rights under the Data Protection Acts and Freedom of Information Act.

Exercises

1. List the rights of individuals under the Data Protection Acts.

2. List the responsibilities of data controllers under the Data Protection Acts.

3. What information is exempt under the Freedom of Information Act?

Bibliography

Ambler, G. 2006. Leadership Lessons from Geese. The Practice of Leadership [online] available at http://www.thepracticeofleadership.net/2006/07/18/leadership-lessons-from-geese/

Ambrose, D. M. and Anstey, J. R. 2007. Better survey design is: (a) easy (b) difficult (c) don't know: stuck for an answer? *ABA Bank Marketing*, 39, 26-31.

Ankeny, J. 2009. How Twitter is revolutionizing business. *Entrepreneur*, 37, 26-32.

Berne, E. See *www.ericberne.com*

Buzan, T. 2006. *Mind mapping*. Harlow, BBC Active.

Conlin, M. 2002. Watch what you put in that office e-mail. *Business Week*, 114-115.

Hartland, D. and Tosh, C. 2001. *Guide to Body Language*. London, Caxton Reference.

Heyman, J. 2004. Five steps create effective online surveys. *Marketing News*, 38, 23-24.

Hopewell, N. 2008. Surveys by design. *Marketing News*, 42.

Kolin, P. 2008. *Successful Writing at Work*. Boston, Houghton Mifflin.

Linehan, M. and Cadogan, T. 2003. *Make that Grade Marketing*. Dublin, Gill and Macmillan.

Manohar, U. 2009. Types of Communication. Buzzle [online] available at http://www.buzzle.com/articles/types-of-communication.html

McClelland, S. B. 1995. *Organizational Needs Assessments: Design, Facilitation, and Analysis*. Westport, Conn., Quorum Books.

McDaniel, C. and Gates, R. 2001. *Marketing Research: the Impact of Internet*. Cincinnati, South-Western.

Mehrabian, A. 2008. *Nonverbal Communication*. New Brunswick, AldineTransaction.

Michaelidou, N. and Dibb, S. 2006. Using email questionnaires for research: Good practice in tackling non-response. *Journal of Targeting, Measurement and Analysis for Marketing*, 14, 289-296.

Mort, S. 1992. *Professional Report Writing*. Aldershot, Brookfield, Vt., Gower.

Newbury, D., Swift, J. 1996. *Presenting Research Findings*. Birmingham Institute of Art and Design, Research Training Initiative.

Nielsen Business Media. 1998. Watch your netiquette. *Successful Meetings*, 47, 36.

O'Neill, S. and Morgan, G. 2007. *Essential Computer Applications: Information and Communication Systems, Databases, Spreadsheets, Word Processing and the Internet*. Dublin, Gill and Macmillan.

Peck, M. S. 1978. *The Road Less Traveled: A New Psychology of Love, Traditional Values, and Spiritual Growth*. New York, Simon and Schuster.

Shah, S. K. and Corley, K. G. 2006. Building better theory by bridging the quantitative–qualitative divide. *Journal of Management Studies*, 43, 1821-1835.

Short Story Writing: First Principles. 2000, 2010. Available at: http://www.literature-study-online.com/creativewriting/first.html. Accessed 17 October 2010.

Singer, M. R. 1998. *Perception and Identity in Intercultural Communication*. Yarmouth, ME, Intercultural Press.

Straus, J. 2008. *The Blue Book of Grammar and Punctuation: An Easy-to-use Guide with Clear Rules, Real-world Examples, and Reproducible Quizzes*. San Francisco, CA, Jossey-Bass.

Tuckman, B. 1965. Developmental sequence in small groups. *Psychological Bulletin*, 63, 384-399.

Wiehardt, G. n.d. How to Write a Short Story, Available at: http://fictionwriting.about.com/od/shortstorywriting/a/shortstoryrules.html. Accessed 17 October 2010.